The Genius Hour Guidebook

Promote your students' creativity and get them excited about learning! In this practical new book, authors Denise Krebs and Gallit Zvi show you how to implement Genius Hour, a time when students can develop their own inquiry-based projects around their passions and take ownership of their work. Brought to you by MiddleWeb and Routledge Eye On Education, the book takes you step by step through planning and teaching Genius Hour. You'll learn how to guide your students as they:

◆ develop inquiry questions based on their interests;
◆ conduct research to learn more about their topic of choice;
◆ create presentations to teach their fellow students in creative ways; and
◆ present their finished product for a final assessment.

At the end of the book, you'll find handy FAQs and ready-made lessons and resources. In addition, a companion website, www.geniushourguide.org, offers bonus materials and regular updates to support you as you implement Genius Hour in your own classroom.

Denise Krebs (@mrsdkrebs) and **Gallit Zvi** (@gallit_z) are co-moderators of the Twitter chat group #geniushour. Denise works in Bahrain, teaching English to kindergarten students in a bilingual Arabic–English school. Gallit is a Faculty Associate in Professional Development Programs at Simon Fraser University, as well as a public school teacher in Surrey, BC.

Other Eye On Education Books, Available from Routledge

(www.routledge.com/eyeoneducation)

STEM by Design:
Strategies and Activities for Grades 4–8
Anne Jolly

The Passion-Driven Classroom:
A Framework for Teaching and Learning
Angela Maiers and Amy Sandvold

Inquiry and Innovation in the Classroom:
Using 20% Time, Genius Hour, and PBL to Drive Student Success
A.J. Juliani

Passionate Learners:
How to Engage and Empower Your Students, 2nd Edition
Pernille Ripp

Connecting Your Students with the World:
Tools and Projects to Make Global Collaboration Come Alive, K–8
Billy Krakower, Paula Naugle, and Jerry Blumengarten

What Connected Educators Do Differently
Todd Whitaker, Jeffrey Zoul, and Jimmy Casas

The 30 Goals Challenge for Teachers:
Small Steps to Transform Your Teaching
Shelly Sanchez Terrell

The Educator's Guide to Writing a Book:
Practical Advice for Teachers and Leaders
Cathie E. West

The Fearless Classroom:
A Practical Guide to Experiential Learning Environments
Joli Barker

Reinventing Writing:
The 9 Tools That Are Changing Writing, Teaching,
and Learning Forever
Vicki Davis

The Genius Hour Guidebook

Fostering Passion, Wonder, and Inquiry in the Classroom

Denise Krebs and Gallit Zvi

Routledge
Taylor & Francis Group

NEW YORK AND LONDON

First published 2016
by Routledge
711 Third Avenue, New York, NY 10017

and by Routledge
2 Park Square, Milton Park, Abingdon, Oxon, OX14 4RN

Routledge is an imprint of the Taylor & Francis Group, an informa business

Library of Congress Cataloging-in-Publication Data
Names: Krebs, Denise, author. | Zvi, Gallit.
Title: The genius hour guidebook : fostering passion, wonder, and
    inquiry in the classroom / by Denise Krebs and Gallit Zvi.
Description: New York ; London : Routledge, [2016] | Includes
    bibliographical references.
Identifiers: LCCN 2015017559| ISBN 9781138937420 (hardback) |
    ISBN 9781138937437 (pbk.) | ISBN 9781315676241 (ebook)
Subjects: LCSH: Inquiry-based learning.
Classification: LCC LB1027.23 .K735 2016 | DDC 371.3—dc23
LC record available at http://lccn.loc.gov/2015017559

ISBN: 978-1-138-93742-0 (hbk)
ISBN: 978-1-138-93743-7 (pbk)
ISBN: 978-1-315-67624-1 (ebk)

Typeset in Palatino
by Swales & Willis Ltd, Exeter, Devon, UK

Dedication

This book is dedicated to all of the amazing students we have had the pleasure of teaching. Your sense of wonder and willingness to try new things inspires us.

Contents

Companion Website

For additional resources on implementing Genius Hour, visit the book's companion website at www.geniushourguide.org.

Brainstorming with Genius Hour group

Meet the Authors

Denise Krebs and Gallit Zvi met on Twitter in 2011 and have been an integral part of each other's PLN since. They've had the joy of meeting face-to-face twice, but most of their collaboration has taken place across many miles.

Denise Krebs is a connected educator, leader and learner. In fact, she is the chief learner in her classroom, whether she's teaching kindergarten or college. Denise has over twenty years' experience in private and public schools and recreation centers in California, Iowa, Michigan, Arizona and Bahrain. Denise's teaching evolved as she began to embrace connected learning for herself and her students. She was teaching junior high when she dove into Genius Hour. Her smart and intrepid junior high students helped her find her way in Genius Hour. Of course, she couldn't have done it without the help of her online PLN and #geniushour community. Today Denise is teaching English to kindergarten geniuses in a bilingual Arabic–English school in Bahrain. Denise tweets at @mrsdkrebs and blogs at *Dare to Care* (http://mrsdkrebs.edublogs.org).

Gallit Zvi is a passionate, connected educator in Surrey, BC with experience teaching fourth through seventh grade in the public school system. She is also a Faculty Associate in the Faculty of Education at Simon Fraser University where she teaches and supervises teacher candidates as they go through the professional development program. Gallit has many years of experience mentoring both teacher candidates as well as experienced teachers and has coached many educators as they implement Genius Hour. Gallit is passionate about helping her students find their passions. She enjoys learning alongside her students and embraces a philosophy of student-centered, inquiry-based and passion-based learning. Gallit tweets at @gallit_z and blogs at *Integrating Technology & Genius Hour: My Journey as a Teacher and Learner* (www.gallitzvi.com).

To the Reader

We hope this book inspires you to take a new risk in your teaching practice and give Genius Hour a try. Or for those of you who have already taken the plunge and are doing Genius Hour with your students, we hope that you find something new to help you and your amazing students along the way.

Thank you for taking this journey with us.

Denise and Gallit met face-to-face in June 2013

Acknowledgments

From Gallit:

I want to thank all of my colleagues and PLN for helping me grow as an educator. Some of you have taught in the same building as me and some inspire me through our online connections, but you are all my critical friends—you cheer me on, challenge me and amaze me with your brilliance. Thank you. A special shout out goes to my former teaching partner, Hugh McDonald: your genuine enthusiasm for learning is awesome! We implemented and tinkered with Genius Hour side by side and developed our practice together. You have helped me grow as an educator and I thank you so much for that. I also would like to thank Antonio Vendramin for encouraging me to be innovative, modeling best practice and pushing me to be the best teacher that I could be.

And a very special thank you to my co-author, Denise Krebs. Who knew that a teacher from the middle of the US and the west coast of Canada would meet online, collaborate virtually and eventually write a book together despite the miles between us? You are amazing, my friend. You teach with all your heart and you inspire me more than you could ever know. I am grateful that we met, became friends and got to write this book together.

I would also like to thank my family and friends for all their love and support. And finally, I want to thank my husband, Johnny Zvi. You live your life like a Genius Hour project: constantly inquiring, learning new things, creating, problem solving and sharing your brilliance with your friends and family. Thank you for supporting me.

From Denise:

I want to say a hearty thank you to Hugh McDonald, too. You were the one who first noticed me sharing with #geniushour on Twitter. Your support made me keep on using the hashtag. Later, my co-author, Gallit Zvi, initiated the #geniushour chat and started the wiki. Thank you, Gallit, for your passionate and capable leadership in building the Genius Hour community, and thank you for writing this book with me. I most certainly wouldn't have done any of these without you. Your passion and encouragement are inspiring, and it has been only a pleasure to work with you.

Another community that shaped me and Genius Hour is Spalding Catholic School. My genius students in the classes of 2016, 2017 and 2018 showed me what they were capable of when invited to learn with autonomy, mastery and purpose. (Thank you, friends. You are great teachers. Go Spartans, Hawks and Jays!) My colleagues and friends, Brenda Ortmann and Mary Hunt, showed me what it meant to become a connected educator. Thank you for introducing me to Twitter and Angela Maiers. Thank you to Kris Full, my friend, teaching partner and fellow dreamer, always willing to listen to all my crazy ideas and share yours with me. I wouldn't be the teacher I am today without you.

I also want to say thank you to my life partner, my husband, Keith. You have believed in me, loved me and served me graciously and generously for 30+ years. Finally, thank you to my two strong, courageous, creative and capable daughters, Maria and Katie—you live life well in the twenty-first century. This one's for you, girls. I love you all.

From both of us:

Both of us would like to say a special thank you to Joy Kirr and Hugh McDonald. When we met via the #geniushour hashtag, we soon became the Fantastic 4, as coined by Vicki Davis when we appeared on the BAM Radio Network. We wrote the Genius Hour Manifesto together for A.J. Juliani, we edited the wiki, we asked each other questions and we shared our journeys. We wouldn't have become the Genius Hour teachers we are without your input.

In addition, we would like to thank all the other amazing teachers who allowed us to share their stories in our book. You are all so inspirational and we have learned so much because of your willingness to share your genius with us. There are so many of you that have chatted with us on the #geniushour hashtag on Twitter or face-to-face at conferences. Thank you all. A special thank you to the teachers whose words and ideas we have highlighted in the book: Robyn Thiessen, Sheri Edwards, Valerie Lees, Paul Solarz, Silvia Rosenthal Tolisano, Jesse McLean, A.J. Juliani, Marianne Smith, Kevin Brookhouser, Lyndsey Own, Kam Grewal, Laura Coughlin, Daniel Lee, Trish Miller, Keith Peters, Katelyn Fraser, Kay Bisaillon, Joel Pardalis, Lindsey Bingley, Melina Louise, Katie Heywood, Oliver Schinkten, Nichole Carter, Laura Verdiel and Craig Dunlap. Space prohibits us from saying thank you to so many more.

A special thank you to Daniel Pink, Sir Ken Robinson, Angela Maiers and Alan November. Your work continues to inspire us. You matter!

Finally, we are indebted to John Norton, from MiddleWeb. You believed in our book when we had begun to lose hope. Thank you for finding a way for this book to become a reality. Thank you so much, Lauren Davis and the whole staff at Routledge. Your work has made this book better than it ever would have been. Together we are smarter.

1

What Is Genius Hour and Why Do Students Need It?

There exists empirical evidence proving that students who are given the freedom to explore areas based on their personal interests, and who are accompanied in their learning by a supportive, understanding facilitator, not only achieve superior academic results but also develop socially and grow personally.

Renate Motschnig[1]

Genius Hour is a precious time, loved by all our students. It is when they are allowed to develop their own inquiry question—about whatever it is that they want to explore. Students develop these questions based on their interests, passions, or even based on something that they are wondering about. For us, it is student-centered learning at its best. Students love it because it gives them the opportunity to learn about the things that they personally wonder about. It is truly personalized learning and so vital because, as one of our students, Morgan, pointed out, "You don't want to learn your teacher's passion, you want to learn your own passion."

Genius Hour provides students time to play with their learning, just like they did when they were in kindergarten. Those young students have no problem asking question after question, as they are truly curious about the world. We want our students to get back in touch with their younger, more inquisitive selves, and we want to guard and nurture their creativity. They can do work important to them without fear of "getting it wrong." Genius Hour allows students to become fearless learners, improving the world.

Genius Hour celebrates their curiosity and gives students time to play with their learning again, time to explore and create. It is time set aside during the school week. When Denise taught junior high, students came for 45-minute classes each day. She gave them 20% of the class time each week to work on their Genius Hour projects. Teachers, like Gallit, in self-contained classrooms, might arrange a block of time once a week for Genius Hour.

During Genius Hour, all the kids are excited and student engagement is at its highest. Some students are huddled around a laptop researching a country they are interested in, others are creating websites or slideshows on an area of interest and some are out in the hallway filming movies. Some aren't using technology at all, but rather are building and creating things with their hands. No matter what they are working on, the common thread is that it is something they are passionate about and/or wonder about.

How We Got Started

So how did we first discover the possibilities of Genius Hour? This idea came to Denise's attention when Angela Maiers tweeted out the idea as she listened to a talk by Daniel Pink. See Figure 1.1.

In a subsequent search, Denise found Daniel Pink's blog post about Genius Hour in a corporate setting. In his blog,[2] he tells of Jen Shefner at the Columbia Credit Union and how each week her "employees can take a Genius Hour—60 minutes to work on new ideas or master new skills. They've used that precious sliver of autonomy well, coming up with a range of innovations including training tools for other branches."

Figure 1.1 The tweet that started Denise thinking about Genius Hour

mrsdkrebs Denise Krebs
I want to hear more! RT @AngelaMaiers: LOVE This! We need to have a **"genius hour"** in school- for teachers and students!
#authorspeak11
22 hours ago

AngelaMaiers Angela Maiers
LOVE This! We need to have a **"genius hour"** in school- for teachers and students! #authorspeak11
23 hours ago

Denise was quick to agree with Pink and came up with a plan to give her seventh and eighth graders their very own Genius Hour. She shared her decision in her own blog, asking others to share their experiences with the #geniushour hashtag.[3] Word started to spread. Gallit is ever so grateful that her teaching partner at the time, Hugh McDonald, retweeted Denise's blog because that is how she "met" Denise. Soon after, Gallit began Genius Hour with her class of fifth and sixth graders and was immediately sold! Gallit also blogged about her experiences with Genius Hour[4] and word continued to spread. (Can you tell we are huge fans of Twitter, blogging and sharing?)

The rest, as they say, is history. The two of us have been incorporating Genius Hour into our classrooms ever since and haven't looked back. Genius Hour has evolved well since those first blog posts we wrote. Since then, we have learned so much. We co-founded the collaborative Genius Hour wiki (http://geniushour.wikispaces.com), where teachers are encouraged to share documents and quotes from their Genius Hour experiences, and we also founded and co-moderate the #geniushour chat on Twitter, where educators gather regularly to have a structured chat about different themes in Genius Hour.

Why Genius Hour Is Worth It

But why spend time doing all of this? Aren't we expected to "cover" enough? How is there time? To answer that question, we first turn to one of our mentors, Sir Ken Robinson. If you haven't yet watched Sir Ken Robinson's Ted Talk about how schools kill creativity, you really should. Here's the link: http://tinyurl.com/TEDcreativity.

Robinson does a fantastic job articulating what so many of us feel. We know something is missing in the way we do school . . . and he helps us articulate it. We completely agree with him when he argues that students *need* to be given opportunities to be creative, and that this is just as important as reading, writing and all the must-haves that we would never dream of overlooking. His point that schools often take the creativity right out of kids is sadly true. A teacher-centered curriculum does not give all students time to explore their own passions, wonders and curiosities.

This is why we love Genius Hour so much. It celebrates and gives students that time to be creative, to *give it a go*, as Robinson says.

Another mentor and inspiration for Genius Hour is the previously mentioned Daniel H. Pink. His blog post about Genius Hour in the business place, his book *Drive* and his Ted Talk all cite evidence that support

Students creating a commercial for the new sport they created during Genius Hour

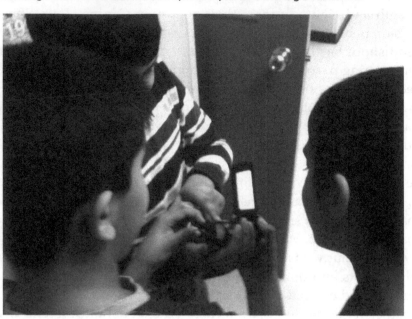

Genius Hour in the classroom. Watch his TED Talk here: http://tinyurl. com/TEDmotivation.

We do Genius Hour in the classroom because human motivation does not come from the teacher telling students what they must learn and then rewarding them with smiley faces and good grades. Indeed, according to Daniel Pink and educational researchers like Alfie Kohn, rewards have an adverse effect on motivation. Teachers know that student motivation is enhanced when autonomy, purpose and mastery are present in the classroom. Motivation comes with autonomy, when students are entrusted with choice and the freedom to make decisions regarding their learning; purpose, when students have a reason for learning what they choose to learn; and mastery, when students are given enough time to actually master and become an expert on what they are learning. It's true for adults, and it's true for children in the classroom.

Companies like Google, 3M and W.L. Gore & Associates have known this.[5] They give employees some room for personal growth, innovation and autonomy. They know that good things emerge if people are given space to be autonomous and work on things they are passionate about—indeed, many of the best innovations come not from management, but from the workers. Or to use an educational analogy, the best learning comes not from the teacher, but directly from the students.

Passion is a huge part of this. In *The Passion Driven Classroom: A Framework for Teaching and Learning*, Angela Maiers and Amy Sandvold talk about the difference between a passion and an interest, explaining that if we are passionate about something, we are willing to give of ourselves for that cause (page 16). We want to help our students find that passion—that thing in life they are so excited about that they would happily devote their time and energy to it, and it wouldn't feel like a burden because it is their passion. We also know that passionate people are successful people. For more on that, watch Richard St. John's Ted Talk on "8 Secrets of Success."[6]

We believe, in order to be successful, students need time to find their passions. Sometimes we assume that kids will know what they are passionate about. We ask things like, "What do you want to be when you grow up?" but really many kids do not know the answer to that question. They may not know what they are passionate about. They need rich and meaningful experiences to help them discover it. That is why we open up Genius Hour to include more than just passions. Students are invited to explore interests and wonders so that they can see if those indeed become passions. Sometimes students will think they have a passion and will start to work on a project and then realize that maybe they aren't so passionate about that after all. That is okay! Better to find out now and explore a new area of interest than to pursue that avenue all through college and then find out that it isn't a good fit.

Genius Hour gives students time to find and follow their passions. It gives them the autonomy to work on their own pet projects. In Genius Hour classrooms, students take charge of their learning and have complete autonomy, giving them purpose to learn and time to move toward mastery. It is passion-based and inquiry-based learning in one.

Benefits for the Learners Doing Genius Hour

- ◆ They have autonomy and purpose.
- ◆ They are given time to master.
- ◆ They make good learning decisions.
- ◆ They become fearless learners.
- ◆ They can stop playing the game of getting good grades.
- ◆ They develop curiosity, innovation and creativity.
- ◆ They explore and wonder to discover their passions.
- ◆ They will be better understood by teacher and peers.
- ◆ They will be instructional leaders as they share their projects.

Crayon art in celebration of Dr. Seuss's birthday and Read Across America Day

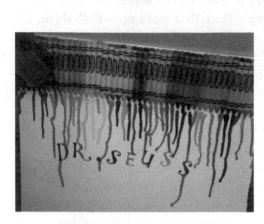

Source: www.flickr.com/photos/mrsdkrebs/6545748251

Genius Hour Takes Classrooms by Storm

As mentioned earlier, the Genius Hour movement has really started to spread—we hear from hundreds of teachers around the world now, and they all have fantastic Genius Hour stories to tell us. Throughout this book, we will share some of the wise words that other Genius Hour educators have shared with us.

For example, Hugh McDonald, a sixth- and seventh-grade teacher, loves Genius Hour. He says:

> I realized the importance of giving students (and myself) autonomous time to be creative and explore their wonders and passions. Students inherently love to learn from a young age, and often they see school as a place that doesn't value what they love to learn. Students shouldn't have to wait to learn something they are curious about. Genius Hour gives them that time.

Similarly, Robyn Thiessen, a third- and fourth-grade teacher, has made Genius Hour a regular part of her teaching. She says:

From our very first Genius Hour session: students learn about baking and decorating a cake

This group loved Genius Hour so much they stayed after school to continue editing their movie

Students' excitement about learning has skyrocketed since I introduced Genius Hour. Students took ownership of their projects, often working for hours on the weekends to complete assignments. Not all students were successful but they learned so much from their failures—resilience, perseverance and grit. This is the time of the week that my students demanded. I chose Wednesday because we were almost always in session, but if we had another commitment, we *had* to reschedule for the next day. Genius Hour time is sacred!

We are so excited that so many teachers are now offering time for their students to do this kind of learning. Every teacher has found their own way to fit it into the curriculum. Of course, the name doesn't matter. Many have called it something unique to fit their purposes. We've heard many different names for this kind of learning, as shown in Table 1.1.

There are a lot of reasons why so many teachers have been implementing Genius Hour in the classroom. Sheri Edwards, an eighth-grade teacher, told us:

What I love about Genius Project Time, besides the joy students discover for learning, is the return to that connected time when I can sit with a student and learn from and about them, building relationships and offering feedback. I'm thankful that my students and I can again dig deeper into class, group or individual sidetracks that meet required objectives *and* passions of students.

We love that Sheri brought up this precious one-on-one time because we feel like that is one of the nicest side benefits of Genius Hour—we get to know our students so well.

Table 1.1 Genius Hour by any other name is still passion-based, student-driven learning

◆ 20% Time	◆ Innovation Week
◆ Personal Learning and Creation Time via Philip McIntosh	◆ Genius Hour
	◆ Boot Leg Time
◆ DIY	◆ SPICE Projects via Jesse McLean
◆ Your Power Hour	◆ REAL-Time Research and Exploration Aimed at Learning via Donna Lasher
◆ Curiosity Friday	
◆ Genius Time Project	◆ Free2Learn Friday – Patti Grayson
◆ Adventure Learning	◆ Passion Time
◆ Passion Project via Paul Solarz	◆ Innovation Day via Josh Stumpenhorst
◆ An Hour of Wonder via Pernille Ripp	◆ 100 Minutes of Genius via Tia Henriksen
◆ Com-passion Project via Oliver Schinkten	◆ Curiosity Friday via Ian Byrd
◆ Google Time	◆ 20 Percent Project
◆ Hack Day	
◆ Genius Time	

Sheri's Story: Using Genius Hour to Develop Passions

Many of the kids at our school are basketball fanatics; they play all year, and they are very good. Why? Because once they get the bug, which is encouraged by their former basketball-playing family members, they want to play all the time. They play all year round and join any team available, from AAU to tribal teams, to their own driveways. They're basketball geniuses because they take the time to learn and improve. That's why Genius Project time is so important—time to find topics that may eventually become a job you love; time to learn a topic, hobby, skill that defines who you are and who you might become; a time to learn and share with classmates and others in the world who share your passions. In short, it builds knowledge, connections and possibilities. And through that passion, students apply all the skills that our standards expect in communication, research, reading, writing, designing, collaboration, media competence, digital citizenship, etc. It defines the reason for school.

The added benefit is better relationships among students and with teachers: learning about each other's passions deepens our understanding of each other as human beings.

From Sheri Edwards, "Genius: It Takes Time" post[7]

Filming a basketball video

Jumping into Your Own Genius Hour

Worried about getting started? Here is some advice from Hugh McDonald about what to do:

> I would say read the stories by educators who regularly blog about Genius Hour [see Chapter 8 of this book—we have already gathered some for you], ask questions [you'll find FAQs and answers at the end this book], jump into the conversation [the conversation never stops on Twitter—check out the #geniushour hashtag], read the wiki[8] to get an idea of resources, try your own Genius Hour project, model it with your students and jump in with two feet. Your students will thank you for it.

 Teacher Tip: Don't Be Afraid to Try Something New!

Change can be scary. It is different, and so it may be uncomfortable, but good stuff can happen when we are a bit uncomfortable—we can grow. Give it a try and be sure to reflect on the process as you go. Then tweak it based on your reflections so that it works for you. Here is a little pep talk from Joy Kirr, a seventh-grade teacher:

> You have a room full of curious, imaginative minds that you need to start utilizing to their fullest potential. If we want them to actually think . . . to make good choices in life, we have to start letting them make choices, fail, adapt and make more choices. You need to be there for them when they do [fail]—as a guide, asking more questions and getting them to think *more*. If you don't give them answers, you can bet that *you* will keep learning along with your students.

Thanks for the pep talks, Hugh and Joy. We couldn't have said it better ourselves!

Summary

Genius Hour is a combination of passion-based and inquiry-based learning. And it is about human motivation. Autonomy, purpose and mastery motivate us. We are inspired by educational leaders such as Sir Ken Robinson who ask us if we are giving students enough time to be creative. Genius Hour gives students time to explore their interests, wonders and passions. It gives them autonomy over their learning and time to be creative and to master tasks they truly care about.

Notes

1 http://tinyurl.com/GHrenate
2 http://tinyurl.com/GHDanPink
3 http://tinyurl.com/GHDenise
4 http://tinyurl.com/GHGallit
5 http://tinyurl.com/WSJideas
6 http://tinyurl.com/TEDsuccess
7 http://tinyurl.com/SheriGenius
8 http://geniushour.wikispaces.com

Introducing Genius Hour to Your Class

Judge a man by his questions rather than by his answers.

Voltaire

Okay, you have heard all about why you should give your students a weekly Genius Hour and you are sold! You see the amazing potential of such a project and you are ready to dive in. But how do you get students started? In this chapter, we will take you through three steps for introducing Genius Hour: Step 1: Inspire Your Class; Step 2: Brainstorm with Students; Step 2.5 (optional): Model and Scaffold; and Step 3: Create an Inquiry Question. Along the way, we'll keep in mind what Parker J. Palmer says, "Good teaching cannot be reduced to technique; good teaching comes from the identity and integrity of the teacher" (Parker J. Palmer, *The Courage to Teach: Exploring the Inner Landscape of a Teacher's Life*). As educators, you will have to do it your way and make it your own, but these are the tried, tested and true ways that have worked for us and many others.

Step 1: Inspire Your Class

First, you will want to inspire learners to prepare to learn whatever they want to. Yes, whatever they want to. Anything. Many students will have a difficult time with that concept, so they will need time to warm up to the idea. They will have questions and need to be encouraged. You may want to take up to two weeks to inspire them with videos such as "Obvious to You. Amazing to Others,"[1] Think Different,"[2] "Caine's Arcade"[3] and "Kid President Pep Talk."[4] We have found these videos to be extremely helpful because they inspire the students, get them thinking and also set us up to have really meaningful discussions.

After we watch a few inspirational videos with our class, we then watch some more practical ones, like "Creativity Requires Time"[5] and "Where Good Ideas Come From."[6] These are excellent because they are natural introductions to what Genius Hour is going to look like. After we watch "Creativity Takes Time," we like to say something like:

> Guess what? I am going to give you that time. That time to be creative and be amazing. That time to do whatever it is that gets you excited. Time to explore your wonders and do things you are passionate about, because that is where brilliance comes from—free time exploring. And then you get to share what you learned, built, created, did.

We use the words of the videos, add some of our own and then ask, "So if you were given this time, what would you do? What would you want to learn about?" This is usually followed by a T/P/S (Think to yourself, Pair up and discuss your thoughts with a partner, and then Share with the rest of the class).

How Hugh McDonald Uses Videos to Inspire

Hugh McDonald describes how he handles this step: "We like to watch inspirational videos, discuss them and connect what bugged the person/ group about their passion and identify the action they took." We love the line of questioning he uses with his students. He gets them to consider what bothered the person about their passion, and then what action they took. Angela Maiers puts it this way, "Don't follow your heart to find your passion, follow your heartbreak." Discussing heartbreaks will certainly help you to have inspiring conversations with your class! Read more about the videos that have inspired Hugh's students at "23 Videos That Sparked Genius Hour Thinking, Collaboration and Actions"[7] and "26 More Videos . . . ."[8]

We love using picture books to inspire as well. Picture books can be used at any grade level and make wonderful hooks to new units—Genius Hour included. Some great books to try are *The Most Magnificent Thing* by Ashley Spires and *What Do You Do with an Idea?* by Kobi Yamada. Picture books are a great way to spark a discussion because they give students an entry point to a class discussion. These two books have messages that are a perfect fit for Genius Hour. You'll find a list of more great Genius Hour picture books in Appendix C.

Another way to inspire our young learners is to take them outside. Learning does not have to happen within the four walls of our classroom. What about a nature walk to help students come up with wonder questions?

Joy Kirr Inspires Through Habitudes and Picture Books

The importance of Step 1 was emphasized by Joy Kirr. When we interviewed her about how she introduced Genius Hour, she explained:

> After much tweaking and reading, we now start with Angela Maiers' idea of "habitudes" [From her book, *Classroom Habitudes*]. I introduce my seventh-grade students to the [habitudes] with picture books. The habitudes of imagination, curiosity, self-awareness, perseverance, courage, passion and adaptability not only set us up for Genius Hour, but also set us up for the culture of the class. I also show two great videos: Kid President's Pep Talk[9] and Caine's Arcade.[10] Our first real venture into Genius Hour starts with the Cardboard Challenge in October. We take our time to set up the "why," so students buy into the "how" later in the year.

Joy introduces Genius Hour to her students every October using the Imagination Foundation's annual Cardboard Challenge, inspired by Caine Monroy's cardboard arcade. Read more about how she does it in this article by Jenny Inglee, which features Joy and her students participating in the Cardboard Challenge: http://tinyurl.com/GHImagination.

Take the time to look at the above examples (or any other inspirational ones you know of) and discuss this precious Genius Hour time with your students. This is key to creating an environment where inquiry is celebrated, learners are honored and a mutual trust is built.

Step 1—this inspiration work—is really important. We have to set up the learning environment so that students know that they are supported and encouraged to be creative. A couple of words of caution here. First, if your classroom is not a safe, creative and inquiring learning environment yet (perhaps it is still early in the school year), spend time studying your class dynamics and making it a place that values questions before you introduce Genius Hour. Then, when it is becoming so, we would also really caution you against just introducing Genius Hour in one session and then sending them off to do the work. Two things could happen. First, Genius Hour becomes a free-for-all and you may choose to abandon it, thinking it's a flawed idea. Second, some students may become paralyzed with the freedom. As Robinson notes in his TED Talk, creativity has been schooled out of most children. We can't just assume they will be amazing because we give them permission to be.

 Teacher Tip: Build Community First!

We know that we have to build community before students can learn; we also believe that we need to foster curiosity and a sense of wonder in our classrooms.

One thing we have realized through discussion with other teachers is that it pays to really establish a sense of community in your classroom before beginning Genius Hour. When we are asking students to take charge of their learning, we are asking them to take a risk, and in order for students to feel safe doing so, there must be a strong sense of community first. Take the time to get to know each other and build trust in your classroom. Students take greater learning risks when they feel safe and supported. In the past, we have built community for a few months into the new school year before introducing Genius Hour to our students.

Step 2: Brainstorm with Students

This takes us to the second step: brainstorming. Students will begin to fashion ideas for Genius Hour. What would they like to learn about, explore or master? This can be done in brainstorming lists that will help them develop inquiry questions for Genius Hour. Ask students to list ten things they love

Figure 2.1 Need help getting ready for Genius Hour? Try these brainstorming ideas

---

Need Help Getting Ready for Genius Hour?

Brainstorm and Find Inspiration:

10 Things You Love to Do and Learn
10 Things You Are Good At
10 Things You Wonder

---

to do, ten things they love to learn, ten things they are good at and ten things they wonder. (See Figure 2.1 for a sample chart, and you'll also find a graphic organizer for student use in Appendix B.)

Not only can students write their individual brainstorming lists, but in many Genius Hour classes they prominently display what they call Wonder Walls or Passion Walls. Any time students think of ideas they are passionate about or wonder, they can add them directly to the wall on a sticky note or white board. These wonderings and passions help inspire not only the person who wrote them, but any other student in the room. Perhaps something on the Wonder Wall will spark an idea for those who have a harder time discovering their Genius Hour inquiry question. See Figure 2.2.

Now, not all of these ideas become good Genius Hour inquiries, but like any brainstorming activity, we like to include every idea. Brainstorms like "I love Joe Jonas Music" may not seem to be a good idea at first, but if a student thinks about it, it can turn into a research project on the life and music of Joe Jonas, or an analysis of how he became famous, etc. Other topics, like "I wonder about physics" certainly have to be narrowed down, but this is a wonderful way to start getting your students thinking about Genius Hour and thinking about their inquiry questions. See Figure 2.3.

Figure 2.2 A Wonder Wall

Figure 2.3 Genius Hour Passion/Wonder Board

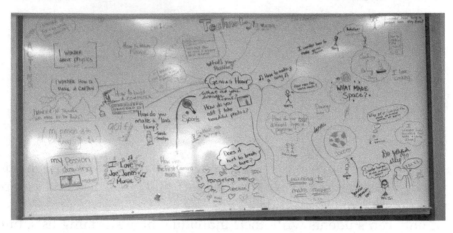

Some students will have ideas immediately. Others will need a little more time to think about it. That is okay . . . and really that is exactly why we are doing this! If your students are having a particularly rough time articulating their passions and wonders, then that is just further proof that they need Genius Hour desperately. Try asking them questions like, "What really bugs you or gets you upset?" This may help them find a cause that they are passionate about. Or ask, "If you could plan a field trip, where would you go?"

If you keep a Wonder Wall in your classroom, when a child does come up with an "I wonder" question, you have a place to document it. If a student asks something during science and there isn't time to answer, put it on the Wonder Wall and encourage them to look into it later. These questions can be thick, rich questions that are good for Genius Hour, or simple research questions that they can Google. It won't take long until students remember the Wonder Wall and add to it when a classroom wonder comes up. No more dismissing questions that are slightly irrelevant or that we don't have time to explore during class time. All of that can still be honored and celebrated by putting it on the Wonder Wall. Students will start to see that curiosity is encouraged in this safe learning place. Similarly, Hugh McDonald says we:

> keep track of and share our wonders and passions on wonder and passion boards in the classroom. After we record these, I guide the students through developing their own essential questions. After the students have developed their questions we jump in.

You might also find that the students who are having a hard time with this are the kids that are usually on track and "good at school." Joy Kirr suggests having a little one-on-one time with these children and asking them, "If you weren't at school right now, what would you be doing?" This not only will lead to some possible Genius Hour topics, but it also helps you get to know your students a little more. In fact, many teachers have shared with us that the best "side-effect" of Genius Hour was getting to know the students on a more personal level, which in turn contributes to a stronger sense of commu- nity in the classroom. That's something we all want.

Kevin Brookhouser, sophomore English teacher at York School in California, suggests the simple question, "How can you help someone else?" This question often helps students who are stuck to think of an idea of ser- vice. Kevin also helps students brainstorm ideas during his "bad idea" factory with his students.[11]

Robyn Thiessen begins her school year with a Me project, in which stu- dents "could use whatever means they desired to share who they were, what they were passionate about as well as what they valued." This was one of her starting points into generating Genius Hour project ideas.

Please do not get disheartened if students cannot identify areas of won- der or passion. This can be hard for so many of our students—they are so used to being told what to do, what to learn about and what to care about. This doesn't mean that Genius Hour will not work for them; in fact, this is precisely why they really need Genius Hour! Students need to practice gen- erating ideas and identifying their own areas of passion and interest. With more practice, they will definitely get better at it.

Step 2.5: Model and Scaffold

We are calling this Step 2.5 because it is optional. Many classes will skip right from Step 2 to Step 3, and that is totally okay. Some classes may want this additional step to scaffold the process before jumping into Step 3 (which is planning the Genius Hour inquiry), so for those that want it, here is Step 2.5.

Step 2.5 will look different in each classroom. If you teach a younger grade, Step 2.5 will probably involve doing a whole-class Genius Hour pro- ject as a way to provide more scaffolding for your younger students.

Most of us begin new projects or units of study with some sort of model- ing process. The gradual release of responsibility model is one that really helps support our learners when learning a new concept, and can also be used when preparing our kids to begin something new, like Genius Hour, espe- cially since so many children aren't used to being creative in the classroom. Students, especially in the older grades, are so used to following directions that Genius Hour may be a bit strange at first. Therefore, taking the time to do Step 2.5 may be beneficial.

Because modeling is so important, a variation of Step 2.5 could include the teacher sharing one of his or her own Genius Hour projects. For example, one year Hugh McDonald and Gallit[12] decided that they would share a wonder they had with their students. They wondered how to create a short iMovie on an iPad (at that time they had never used the iMovie app on an iPad before). So they shared their inquiry question with the class and then went home and used Canadian Thanksgiving weekend as the inspiration to create their own Genius Hour projects. When they returned to school the following week, they shared their videos with the class, and talked about their learning process and how they overcame obstacles (like splitting clips). Voila! A sample Genius Hour project so that all students had some sort of reference point for their own projects.

Whether you do Step 2.5 or not is up to you. You know your students best and what works for them. Gallit always leans toward more modeling and more scaffolding, but it really is your choice. Your students may be too excited and just want to start already. So then go ahead. But it would still be cool to do your own Genius Hour project and share it with your class. Students love getting to know more about their teachers. This is a fantastic way to share your passions and wonders with your students. In fact, share it with all of us, using the #geniushour hashtag on Twitter. We would love to see your project.

Step 3: Create an Inquiry Question

So, at this point it is really tempting to just say "go" and have the kids start their projects, and truthfully that is what we did the first time with our students too. However, we have found that having an inquiry question is more beneficial than just having a topic. So the final step in introducing Genius Hour to your class is to have each student come up with an inquiry question. Many teachers have asked us if it is okay for students to pair up during Genius Hour. We think it is. We would allow students to work in partners or small groups if they had the same area of interest, wonder or passion. Denise limits group size to three so that everyone stays engaged. If four or five are interested in the same project, they can then split into smaller groups and still keep their idea. These students then formulate their inquiry question together.

This might be a great time to connect to language arts if you are teaching the art of questioning as a reading comprehension strategy. We want our students to ask deep questions, meaningful questions.

A couple of years ago when we contributed to *The Best and Next in Education*,[13] Gallit said:

> In a time when answers to fact-based questions are so easily "Google-able," shouldn't we be encouraging our students to create, innovate and ask deep, meaningful questions? I don't need my students to memorize dates and facts. I want them to push the boundaries of their imaginations and become creative doers who fully believe themselves capable of genius, because indeed they all are.

This definitely relates to this third step—take the time to teach your students the difference between a Google-able question and a thick (non Google-able) question. If you haven't already discussed this as a class in another subject area, then it is worth addressing before students create their Genius Hour inquiry question.

What's a Non Google-able Question?

Ewan McIntosh suggests a simple activity to help students discuss the difference between Google-able and non Google-able questions.[14] Students first brainstorm questions from their books and classroom curriculum (or questions of interest to them for Genius Hour projects). Then they separate the questions into two headings: Google-able and non Google-able. Teachers can help students figure out features of non Google-able questions in order to generate more. Google-able questions can be easily researched by students and reported back to the class, with students as teachers. The non Google-able questions can become the rich basis for Genius Hour projects.

In Appendix B, you'll find five lesson plans about helping children with inquiry questions. To give you an idea, here are a few Genius Hour inquiry questions from our classes:

1. How can we spread happiness around our school?
2. What were some of the main events in World War 2?
3. How do you make a pinhole camera?
4. How does Green Screen technology work?
5. How can we make Monday mornings happier for commuters in our neighborhood? (inspired by Sophia Pink's short film)

6. Which art medium do I prefer?
7. How do you make a stop motion movie?
8. How do you create a video game?
9. What's a good way to make a Minecraft creation into a video to share on YouTube?
10. What cool effects can we add to an iMovie?
11. Can we tell a story without telling the story with words?
12. I want to be a teacher when I grow up. After interviewing and observing some teachers at our school, which grade would I prefer? Why?
13. How do hydraulic systems work? How can I make a model hydraulic system?
14. How can we create something to help junior highers survive junior high?
15. Can I write a funny script for a play or movie?
16. How do you do magic tricks?

Teacher Tip: Supporting Those Who Can't Come Up with an Inquiry Question

If someone is having trouble, we would recommend going back to Step 2: Brainstorm, and work through that step one-on-one with that student. It will only take a few minutes and could make all the difference. If you have a Wonder Wall or Passion Board (see Figures 2.2 and 2.3), you could look at it with the student and ask her/him if any of the things on that wall interest them, or perhaps something reminds him/her of a similar interest. Some students have a hard time with open-ended questions at first and may need to borrow a classmate's idea. Over time, they will learn to come up with their own questions.

Summary

We believe that in order for Genius Hour to be successful, it has to be introduced properly, using the steps outlined in this chapter: Inspire, Brainstorm, Model and Scaffold, Create. But as we have said, you need to make this process your own. You know what you are comfortable with and what your students need. This is the framework that we use and we encourage you to follow the steps laid out, but we also want you to make them your own. As you know, teaching is a very personal and complex art—there is no one way to do things. Have fun with your students. Celebrate curiosity and creativity. Let them explore.

Notes

 1 http://tinyurl.com/GHObvious
 2 http://tinyurl.com/GHDifferent
 3 http://tinyurl.com/GHCaine
 4 http://tinyurl.com/GHPepTalk
 5 http://tinyurl.com/GHTime
 6 http://tinyurl.com/GHGoodIdeas
 7 http://tinyurl.com/GHVideos1
 8 http://tinyurl.com/GHVideos2
 9 http://tinyurl.com/GHPepTalk
10 http://tinyurl.com/GHCaine
11 http://tinyurl.com/GHBadideas
12 http://tinyurl.com/GHModel
13 Read the book here: https://leanpub.com/bestandnextineducation
14 http://tinyurl.com/GHGoogleable

3

The Launch: Diving In and Letting Go

The principal goal of education is to create individuals who are capable of doing new things, not simply of repeating what other generations have done.

Jean Piaget

Now that you have been establishing a learning environment of mutual trust and wonder, *and* your students have their inquiry questions, you are ready to have students dive into their work. Students should follow these four steps, which we'll roll out over the next few chapters:

◆ The Launch: Diving in and Letting Go (Chapter 3);
◆ Loosening Deadlines and Sharing Passions (Chapter 4);
◆ Helping Kids Make Their Learning Visible (Chapter 5);
◆ Teaching about Self-Assessment and Feedback (Chapter 6).

Note that these steps are not numbered. Unlike the first three steps you read about in the last chapter, these four don't always go in a particular order. Often our students will be working on all the steps during one session and certainly not all of your class will be doing the same step at the same time. These steps are completely student-centered and at their own pace, unlike Steps 1–3, which are still fairly teacher-directed and involve the whole class doing the same sort of thing at the same time.

Can You Learn to Love Letting Go?

In this chapter, we talk about diving in and letting go—not an easy thing for teachers trained to manage and control learning at all times! As you read, we hope you will find the strength to let go. This is important, so we are going to repeat it: *Let go*. Teachers are so used to being in charge. It is the way we were taught, and the way many people expect us to perform. In the past, when we think of a teacher, we picture a grown-up standing at the front of the room teaching his/her students. We are asking you to let go of that idea of a teacher. We are asking you, instead, to consider taking off your "expert" hat, and becoming the guide instead. Actually, you need to become more than a guide. You become a fellow learner. According to Donald Graves, "the teacher is the chief learner in the classroom." For Genius Hour, allow your students to take control of their own learning and, instead of teaching, walk around the room and witness your students learning on their own (or in their partnerships/small groups). Learn with them. Learn from them. Sometimes it is hard to let go of control, but when you do, amazing things will happen.

This truly is the time to let the students take charge of the learning and become the decision makers. Things may seem a bit chaotic to you at first because not everyone is doing the same thing at the same time. Some students will be researching, some will be inventing and others will be documenting and reflecting. Everyone will be working at their own pace on an area of their passion or their wonder.

During Genius Hour, students are assessed for learning (more on this in Chapter 6). The teacher is always present to offer suggestions and help, encouragement and redirection as necessary. The assignment itself, however, is coming from the learner's passion and interest, so they are usually motivated to have encouragement through the process. They will also teach you a few things about their passion. Formative assessments can be accomplished through one-on-one conferences, group discussions, peer feedback and self-evaluations. You will absolutely love running around the classroom during Genius Hour and hearing your students share their passions and interests with you! Your students will love your interest and enthusiasm about their passions too.

You Can Still Lay Down Some Ground Rules

It's good to lay down a few ground rules for Genius Hour. We asked some Genius Hour veterans what rules they have for this special choice-filled time. Hugh McDonald explained that his "rules" are that students choose their project, they choose when they are ready to present and they are asked to

Remote control car racing and video recording in the gym

share their learning in a visible way. The teacher gives autonomous time to practice being resilient and explore their own learning questions. "It is amazing to watch the transformation of a shy and struggling learner who regularly reads their presentation to a proud and confident one who smiles and shares their learning," he says. Yes, that is an amazing by-product of having your students follow rules such as these.

Another innovative Genius Hour teacher, Sheri Edwards, says that she asks her students to create, contribute, communicate, consider, cooperate, collaborate and curate successfully. What could be more important for success in this century? How does she do this? She has incorporated two rules of improv from Randy Nelson, Director at Apple University. The rules are:[1]

1. Accept every offer (for help, advice, constructive criticism, anything).
2. Make your partner look good (partner = your classmate, your parents, your teacher, a blogger, an author, etc.).

Joy Kirr has three simple rules for her students each week when she gives them Genius Hour time: "I tell students they may read, write, or create."

Daniel Lee, a grades 3 and 4 teacher in Surrey, British Columbia, came up with the brilliant "IDEAS" acronym (invention, design, experiment, act, share) for his class. Then Trish Miller, also an elementary teacher at the same school, used it in her classroom because it helped her young students who needed more guidance about what to do during Genius Hour. In her words, IDEAS provided her students with "a springboard to get kids thinking of ways they could represent their passions and interests." See Figure 3.1.

Guide Students through Their Research (But Don't Require It)

Some teachers insist that student Genius Hour projects must include some sort of research component. We have never made this a part of our "Genius

Figure 3.1 IDEAS acronym may help students focus during Genius Hour

Source: www.flickr.com/photos/mrsdkrebs/14625360713

Hour rules" as we do not want to discourage our students who are working on an inquiry project that is more about creating than researching. However, many students will rely on some sort of research process for their Genius Hour project and for that we would like to suggest the use of the KWHLAQ chart (see Figure 3.2). You have heard of a KWL chart before—well, this is similar and, no, we didn't just accidentally hit the keyboard with our elbow. It is meant to have all those letters! It is much more detailed than your old KWL.

We love this beautiful alternative to the KWL chart. Paul Solarz, Illinois elementary school teacher and author of *Learn Like a Pirate*, has used the KWHLAQ chart created by Silvia Rosenthal Tolisano to guide student inquiry. Read Silvia's post from 2011, "Upgrade Your KWL Chart to the 21st Century,"[2] and Paul's use of it in his Passion Time projects with his fifth-grade geniuses: "Creating Passion Projects (Genius Hour)."[3] Silvia has shared the KWHLAQ chart on Flickr[4] with this Creative Commons license, CC-BY-NC-SA-2.0 (which means that you are free to use, copy, remix and redistribute this KWHLAQ chart for non-commercial uses with a share-alike license—just make sure you attribute the original KWHLAQ chart to Silvia).

Figure 3.2 KWHLAQ chart

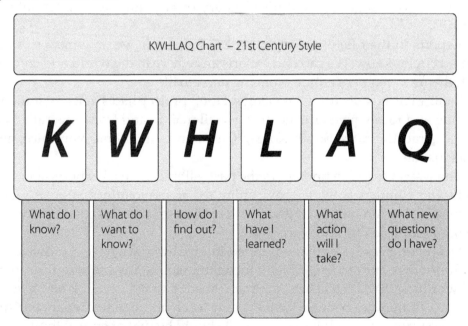

KWHLAQ Chart – 21st Century Style

K W H L A Q

K	W	H	L	A	Q
What do I know?	What do I want to know?	How do I find out?	What have I learned?	What action will I take?	What new questions do I have?

Source: Used with permission of Silvia Rosenthal Tolisano (@Langwitches); www.flickr.com/photos/langwitches/5958295132

Don't Assume Students Know How to Find *Good* Information

The KWHLAQ chart is used to organize twenty-first-century learning. Students record what they know, what they wonder and what they've learned, just like the traditional KWL chart. Sandwiched in between, though, is an important piece on *how*. How will I research and find out what I wonder about and want to know? To teach the *how* is a much more complicated process now than it was for many teachers when we were young students. How did we find out decades ago? We went to the library and looked it up in an encyclopedia or in professionally vetted nonfiction books. If we were at home, we could call the library, and the librarian would use those same resources to find the information we needed. If we knew an expert, we could talk to her or him. Or we could write a letter and send it in the very slow mail, which Denise did on occasion, like when she sent a letter to Australia to ask for information about her country report, for instance.

Now, there was nothing wrong with those ways to find out. In fact, we still use them with great success. Librarians were great researchers. They still are, but now we can talk to librarians anywhere in the world. We no longer have to rely on the nonfiction book collection curated by our small-town librarians, but we have the world's libraries open to us. With a quick question on Twitter, we can talk to librarians at the New York Public Library, the Library of Congress, the British Library or any number of international libraries.

Experts in their field no longer have to be people we or someone in our limited circles know. We can find experts anywhere in the world and connect with them via Skype, Twitter, blogging and email.

Snail mail is still fun. One Genius Hour project had Denise's students sending and receiving chocolate[5] using snail mail to and from Australia,[6] the United Arab Emirates, South Korea,[7] China and Argentina. Very nice, and delicious too!

The ways we had to find out in the past—libraries, local experts and snail mail—were limited. Now, we have unlimited access to information. A world of amazing learning for us is always at our fingertips. It has changed forever the nature of teaching and learning.

However, because of that unlimited information, we have a problem. So much of what our students might encounter can be inaccurate, misleading and worthless. We, as teachers, are more needed than ever. In *Who Owns the Learning*, Alan November says, "If we only teach one skill to prepare our students to survive in a web-based world, it should be that of critical thinking in the analysis of online information."

We are in an excellent position during Genius Hour to teach children and young people how to find out, how to think critically and how to analyze online information. We can teach them how to find reliable sources from multiple perspectives, so they can begin to solve real-world problems. Genuine mini-lessons on these and other topics emerge during authentic researching experiences in Genius Hour.

Alan November shares a story about a high school student who got an A on a paper about the Iranian hostage crisis. The student reported that all of his sources were obtained from the Internet. When November asked the student to show him how he had found his sources, November challenged him on the fact that he didn't search for sources from Iran. In fact, this high school A student didn't even know how to search using the root zone for a country, in this case [site:ir]: much less did he know what the Iranian hostage crisis would have been called in Iran.[8]

Teachers, we are needed more than ever to guide our students in *how* to find out.

Help Students Turn Research into Action

Don't forget the *Action* column of the twenty-first-century KWHLAQ chart: "What action will I take?" When Denise first tried the KWHLAQ chart, it was during science class with seventh graders. In a genetics unit, she asked students to complete the KWHLAQ chart, and she was so excited to see them take seriously the *Action* column. Students began to create and dream about how they could take action in fighting genetic diseases. You can read more about student action improving the world in Chapter 7.

Let Students Take Advantage of the Freedom

People often ask if the students have trouble staying on task. To those people we say a resounding, "No, they do not have trouble staying on task." (However, as most teachers can attest, they sometimes do when we aren't in Genius Hour, when we are dictating the agenda.)

Skeptics and future Genius Hour teachers alike also ask, "Do students take advantage of the freedom?" "Yes, fully!" we say with enthusiasm. They love the learning environment during Genius Hour. They use every moment wisely.

In fact, one of Denise's favorite things during our first whole-morning Genius Hour block was when the bell rang after the first period. (The bells continued to ring because the high school students were in regular classes that morning.) Initially, when students heard the bell, Denise saw the look of disappointment on their faces. Then a look of sunshine and delighted cries of "Ooh, we don't have to leave!" (Chances are that most of us don't normally hear that kind of reaction at the end of a first-period class.) All morning long, through four class periods, students worked on their Genius Hour projects— they happily continued to learn, ignoring bells and only taking occasional bathroom breaks.

Now, to be sure, we know what people *really* mean when they ask, "Do they take 'advantage' of the freedom?" They mean, "Do students mess around and waste time, instead of learning on their own?" To that we can both answer, "Absolutely not." They have purpose. They have chosen what they want to learn; no one dictated it. They are given freedom to take as long as is needed to be satisfied with their learning. For many students, whatever time they are given is not enough. They work on their Genius Hour projects during study halls, before school, at home and during recesses. They are passionate because they have chosen purposeful learning.

 Teacher Tip: What If One or Two Students Are Just Not Engaged?

Joy Kirr dealt with this when she tweeted out an image of a student evaluation she received. See Figure 3.3. We will always have struggling students with us. Even in Genius Hour. When she saw this picture, Kay Basilion said in a tweet that it's so easy to dismiss 99 raving compliments and focus on one criticism, but that the issue was definitely worth a conversation.[9]

Joy agreed and organized a Google Hangout (GHO) for those educators who wanted to have that conversation. We both participated in that GHO and spent over an hour discussing this important topic. You can see the discussion notes and linked ideas on the Google document[10] created before, during and after the GHO.

A lot of good points were made about engaging our students who struggle with Genius Hour. It is important to point out that we all agreed that it really is just a tiny percentage of students who struggle with Genius Hour, and that no matter what we are teaching that is usually the case. Also important to note is that it tends to be a different group of students who struggle in this area—don't be surprised if it isn't your usual student(s) to whom you typically need to provide additional support.

Figure 3.3 What about the one student who isn't engaged?

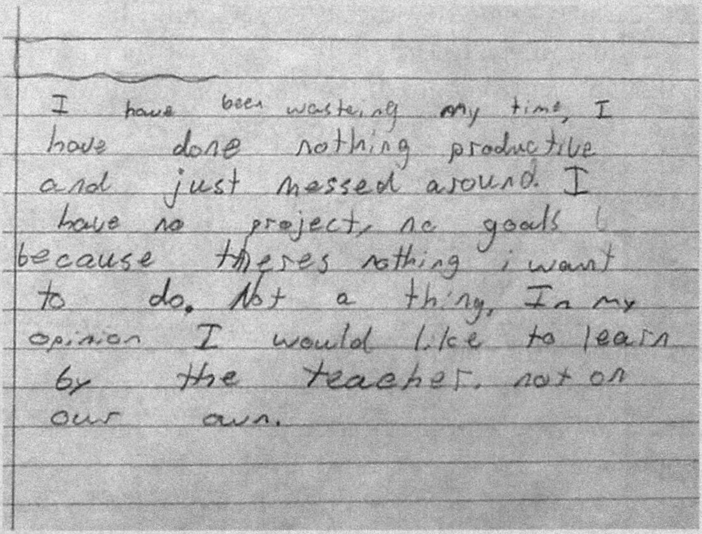
I have been wasteing my time, I have done nothing productive and just messed around. I have no project, no goals because theres nothing i want to do. Not a thing, In my opinion I would like to learn by the teacher. not on our own.

Source: https://twitter.com/JoyKirr/status/468933288699363330

During the chat, Elizabeth Monroe suggested beginning with acknowledging that the student was having a rough go at things, or perhaps had done nothing even, and saying something along the lines of "How do we move on from here?" We love that she doesn't dwell on the negative and instead is looking forward with her student.

Joy Kirr suggested saying something along the lines of "I noticed that ___, and here's my challenge to you____" Again, we love that she is helping the student think forward. It is all about a growth mindset really. During the chat, Charlene Doland mentioned that "we need to model a growth mindset" and she suggested the book *Mindset* by Carol Dweck.

(continued)

(continued)

Hugh McDonald added that an excellent place to start is by getting in the habit of saying "yet." So instead of saying "I don't know how to code," we are modeling and encouraging our students to say "I don't know how to code *yet*." This fits in brilliantly with Genius Hour, as we are all about growing and developing our areas of passion.

It is also worth mentioning that sometimes we worry that our students aren't learning enough and that there should be more evidence of growth, but that doesn't necessarily mean that they aren't learning and growing. Sometimes the tip of the iceberg is just that, and we cannot see what is happening underneath the water. Hugh McDonald has noted about his class that he "noticed engaged learners loving what they were doing" but that he also thought some students were certainly more prepared than other students were. Even in those situations when students were less prepared, he was able to see those few students had "an improved awareness of themselves as learners." We love that he took the time to mention this to us. Metacognition, or knowing how we come to know something, is so important. Even if the project was a bust, learning about the way you learn is definitely worth celebrating. The more we know about the way we learn, the better we can learn moving forward. Added bonus: metacognition[11] is a standard that our students can and need to learn (Common Core State Standards, British Columbia Learning Standards and more).

Remember: When You Let Go, You Naturally Differentiate Instruction

Genius Hour helps children personalize their own learning. With Genius Hour, all children in a class, whether gifted or developmentally delayed, will have at least part of their school week when their learning is perfectly fitted to them. Teachers who strive to differentiate for all students can enjoy this Genius Hour time when students themselves choose what to do based on their readiness, interest and learning profile. They choose the content, the process and what product to show their learning. As students are allowed to personalize their own learning, their teachers will watch and learn. They will become better at differentiating for their students.

Genius Hour and Differentiation: A Student in the Special Education Program Shares His Passion

Here's a story that represents many of our students who need to have Genius Hour.

Denise met a new friend while substitute teaching a while back. His name is Jason.[12] The first time she met him, he was struggling through his seventh-grade math assignment. She was the substitute teacher in a special needs classroom, and she was asked to help him make sense of his math homework during study hall.

Guiding Principle #5 in the Special Education Eligibility Standards[13] says that the State of Iowa has adopted the position that disability labels are not to be used in the education setting. It goes on to explain that a label doesn't identify a child's special needs or provide educators with information to help meet the child's instructional needs. A label mistakenly may suggest that children who share the same label will have the same characteristics. Labels are negative and may be permanently stigmatizing. A label can influence a teacher or school to expect less of the individual or give a more restrictive environment than is needed.

All true, but Denise wishes the guiding principle would also state that a label doesn't identify a child's special strengths.

Her friend Jason has no label, but he does have an intellectual disability that requires significant modifications in school, and his disability made these geometry problems out of reach for him in the traditional way he was being asked to complete them. However, he also has special strengths that Denise was glad she took time to learn about.

After study hall, it was time for literature. They began with independent reading. Denise noticed Jason was intently reading an informational book about farm equipment. It was rich with images, sidebars and facts, and it was interesting enough that Jason was transfixed for the whole reading time.

When the independent reading was up, Denise veered away from the lesson plan the teacher had left. Instead of asking Jason to use Quizlet to practice a more-social-studies-vocabulary-words-than-anyone-should-ever-give-any-seventh-grader-in-one-sitting list, Denise asked Jason to tell her about farm equipment.

He could have talked all day very articulately about all kinds of farm equipment—antique and modern. She asked him many questions, which he gladly answered. They had a lively discussion. She was interested in how corn rows used to be planted farther apart. They got out a meter stick and measured 30", 20" and more widths of corn rows. He told her how wide he and his dad planted corn. More corn can now grow on the same amount of land so the yield is higher than it used to be, he explained.

They measured how close each seed is usually planted. He told her you have to be careful not to get the plants too close together—no closer than four inches. They need "elbow room," he said, so they can get enough sun on their leaves. They actively applied math and science. No longer recognizable as traditional teacher and student, they were two teachers and two learners.

For just twenty minutes, she shunned the written lesson plan and let Jason show off his unique strengths. Other students in this same special education room took notice and listened. It was the first time he was the educational leader in the classroom that day.

Prior to this exchange, Denise had grown weary of this long day, where she helped special needs students find answers in ten-pound textbooks and write those meaningless content answers on notebook paper in painful, laborious manuscript writing. She hated listening to students read orally from chapter books many years above their reading level. She disliked the charade of helping students study vocabulary words that they couldn't pronounce, nor could they even read the words in the stale dictionary definitions, much less understand the meaning. The lessons she was asked to teach were considered "modified" lessons of the general education curricula, which in reality were just less of the same material the general education students were doing. She didn't believe they were modified, as the guiding principle suggests, "to meet the instructional needs of the student."

If she was discouraged during this day, she wondered, how much more so must the children be discouraged? They constantly face an uphill battle. She never once saw, "A-ha! Eureka! I get it. Now let me finish independently." Shouldn't that happen at least once during a school day?

Therefore, giving Jason twenty minutes to learn and teach about his passion was definitely the best part of her day, and she would guess it was a pretty good part of Jason's day too.

Her hope is that someday she will witness Jason, along with his "regular" education peers, participating in Genius Hour. She envisions him voraciously reading and learning even more about farm equipment. She can almost hear him present his farming expertise to his peers and teachers. She can see his surprised friends and teachers authentically applauding for Jason when he finishes, and she delights in the look of pride on Jason's face. Genius Hour is a great fit for all students.

Summary

As much as we believe you will love setting up Genius Hour with your class (watching those inspirational videos, sharing passions and wonders), we also think you will love the time spent on Genius Hour each week. Your students will be engaged as they work on their inquiry projects and you will learn so much about each of your students while they work on their projects, self-assess and share their genius with the class. In fact, many teachers—and we concur—express that they felt they truly got to know their students because of Genius Hour.

Notes

1 http://tinyurl.com/GHImprov
2 http://tinyurl.com/UpdateKWL
3 http://tinyurl.com/GHPaul
4 http://tinyurl.com/GHchart
5 http://tinyurl.com/GHIowa
6 http://tinyurl.com/GHAustralia
7 http://tinyurl.com/GHKorea
8 http://tinyurl.com/WhoOwnsLearning and http://tinyurl.com/GH6Questions
9 https://twitter.com/KayBisaillon/status/468938937000816642
10 http://tinyurl.com/GHOScaffolding
11 http://tinyurl.com/GHMeta
12 Name and details have been changed.
13 http://tinyurl.com/SPED5, page 3.

Loosening Deadlines and Sharing Passions

Creativity now is as important in education as literacy, and we should treat it with the same status.

Sir Ken Robinson

When we began to do Genius Hour with our classes, we set deadlines. We told students how long their self-selected inquiry projects would go. Yes, we said three weeks to research and plan a presentation. Then the fourth week, everyone shared. Another time we had a special three-hour Genius Hour, and then everyone presented in the fourth hour. It worked for many students, but, of course, some students needed more time, as they were not finished inquiring about their topic. Our deadlines evolved quickly to a philosophy of "Finish when you finish. Share when you are ready."

Require Presentations at the End, Whenever That May Be

In our classrooms now, no matter how long they choose to work on a given topic, after they finish, a presentation is required. We expect our students to share their newfound learning with the rest of the class. We want them to

Figure 4.1 Genius Hour presentation ideas

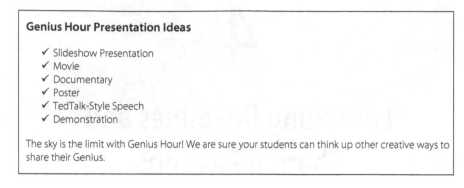

Genius Hour Presentation Ideas

✓ Slideshow Presentation
✓ Movie
✓ Documentary
✓ Poster
✓ TedTalk-Style Speech
✓ Demonstration

The sky is the limit with Genius Hour! We are sure your students can think up other creative ways to share their Genius.

share their genius with their classmates, and beyond, when possible. And, the best part, they *want* to share their passions. As a result, the sharing is rich, personal, real.

We have had students share by talking to us about their project, sharing a demonstration, making a presentation slideshow and even creating a documentary about the process. See more options for sharing in Figure 4.1.

If you have students who are afraid to speak in front of the class, then they may love creating documentaries. This way, they can make the movie in private and then all they have to do in class is hit play on the computer. Shy students will become empowered when they are sharing about something that matters to them. (See high school English teacher Valerie Lees' inspiring tweet in Figure 4.2.)

Figure 4.2 Tweet by Valerie Lees

Valerie Lees
@v_lees

🔽 Following

Getting excited for #geniushour pres. Next week #fhlearn Quietest kid in class wants 30-40 min to present! Beyond any other class pres!

← Reply   ⟲ Retweeted   ★ Favorite   ●●● More

Source: https://twitter.com/v_lees/status/332535105799213056

In Marianne Smith's classroom, students were excited to present their Genius Hour projects. Marianne reflected:

> On week five I casually asked my students who wanted to present their genius next week (they had been reminded that I was not marking their presentations). Without hesitation every student (but one) raised his/her hand. They were incredibly excited to share their genius with the class. The following Friday the students presented and their presentations were effective and engaging. They didn't appear to be nervous because this was something they chose to do. As a teacher I had never witnessed the majority of the class being so excited to present in front of their peers before.[1]

We love how Genius Hour gave her students courage. They were willing to be vulnerable in order to share their projects—passionate learners indeed!

As you'll see when you implement Genius Hour in your own classroom, students will enjoy sharing, and the audience will enjoy listening. You will find students signing up for longer Genius Hour presentation times than they would ever need for, let's say, a history presentation. Katherine Heywood shares a powerful moment in Figure 4.3.

Help Students Notice and Practice Good Presentation Habits

During Genius Hour presentations, students can practice giving and receiving feedback among classmates. Not only are students motivated to learn, but they also want to learn to be more effective presenters. Their peers can help them improve their presentation skills with their constructive feedback. Students can do something as simple as writing one "praise" and one

Figure 4.3 Tweet by Katherine Heywood

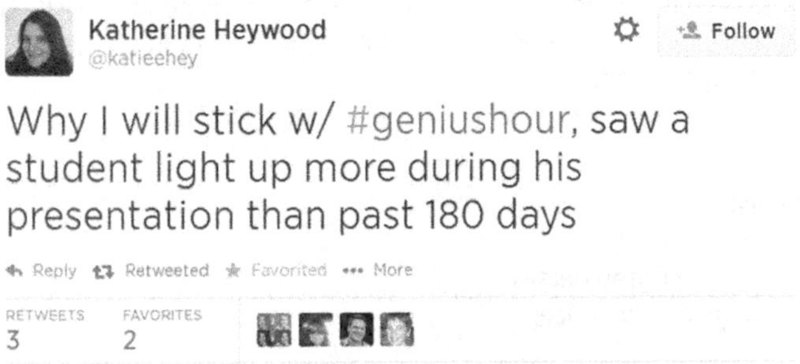

Katherine Heywood
@katieehey   ⚙ Follow

Why I will stick w/ #geniushour, saw a
student light up more during his
presentation than past 180 days

↩ Reply ⟲ Retweeted ★ Favorited ••• More

RETWEETS   FAVORITES
3   2

Source: https://twitter.com/katieehey/status/340266043136172032

"polish" (or a star and a wish—whatever lingo you prefer) for each student presentation. Table 4.1 shows key presentation skills that students will hone during Genius Hour. These skills meet the Common Core State Standards and other rigorous standards.

Of course, not every student will be practicing every standard for each Genius Hour project all of the time, but you can clearly see how Genius Hour is a wonderful way to practice these standards.

Table 4.1 Key presentation skills

Presentations

Because students finishing up their Genius Hour projects *want* to present their knowledge and ideas, it is prime time for them to practice good presentation habits. Here are some sample Common Core State Standards in fourth and seventh grades that students can practice while presenting.

Presentation of Knowledge and Ideas	Presentation of Knowledge and Ideas
CCSS.ELA-LITERACY.SL.4.4 Report on a topic or text, tell a story or recount an experience in an organized manner, using appropriate facts and relevant, descriptive details to support main ideas or themes; speak clearly at an understandable pace.	CCSS.ELA-LITERACY.SL.7.4 Present claims and findings, emphasizing salient points in a focused, coherent manner with pertinent descriptions, facts, details and examples; use appropriate eye contact, adequate volume and clear pronunciation.
CCSS.ELA-LITERACY.SL.4.5 Add audio recordings and visual displays to presentations when appropriate to enhance the development of main ideas or themes.	CCSS.ELA-LITERACY.SL.7.5 Include multimedia components and visual displays in presentations to clarify claims and findings and emphasize salient points.
CCSS.ELA-LITERACY.SL.4.6 Differentiate between contexts that call for formal English (e.g., presenting ideas) and situations where informal discourse is appropriate (e.g., small-group discussion); use formal English when appropriate to task and situation. (See grade 4 Language standards 1 for specific expectations.)	CCSS.ELA-LITERACY.SL.7.6 Adapt speech to a variety of contexts and tasks, demonstrating command of formal English when indicated or appropriate. (See grade 7 Language standards 1 and 3 for specific expectations.)

So, what might a teacher expect in a child's presentation?

Students should always practice well. Even if they are not being graded—and we hope they are not—they can be expected to practice good standards-based presentation skills. They should be familiar with your curriculum's standards for presentations and be attempting to practice these at a developmentally appropriate level.

Whether their presentation is done live for an audience or taped earlier, students should all strive for a presentation that includes:

◆ valid and reliable information;
◆ helpful organization;
◆ essential, carefully chosen details;
◆ a plan to engage the audience;
◆ cited sources;
◆ interesting visual effects and media;
◆ effective oral presentation (diction, pronunciation, volume, etc.).

Teacher Tip: How Do You Fit in the Presentations and Keep Them from Getting Too Long?

Now, we can probably all agree that this is a problem we would like to have: students so keen to share their learning that we just don't know how to schedule them all in. At times during regular school, we've noticed students may hope that we forget to call on them to make the presentation that is due that day. Or they watch the clock, begging it to speed up, so the class will be over before they have to get up and make that science presentation. For Genius Hour presentations, however, the opposite is true. More often students ask if they can present. In addition, their peers are excited for them to present because they have been in the same room seeing them work on their projects of interest. So we have to make sure we keep the length of their presentations on track. Some teachers have students sign up for one, two or three five-minute slots. The students decide how long they will need. Joy Kirr says that her students benefit from the use of timer signs as well as "louder" signs to help coach presenters during the process. There are free timer apps that you can use on your tablet that may help too. Students should learn to limit their presentations to the time they were allotted. Figure 4.4 shows an example of a two-minute warning poster, which can be held up at the appropriate time by the designated time keeper.

Figure 4.4 Idea for a two-minute warning sign

Source: www.keepcalm-o-matlc.co.uk/p/keep-calm-but-this-is-your-2-minute-warning

Remember That Students Are Building Key Twenty-First-Century Competencies

It is amazing how many twenty-first-century competencies can be practiced during Genius Hour. The International Society for Technology in Education (ISTE) has identified key standards for students (see Figure 4.5).

We cannot think of a better way to explore these standards, and to practice them—we mean really practice them—in an authentic and meaningful way, than Genius Hour. Genius Hour is a beautiful fit for students to authentically work on their twenty-first-century skills. Let's take a look at each ISTE standard listed in Figure 4.5 and see how.

Creativity and Innovation

Since students design their own Genius Hour questions, the creativity starts right from the beginning. Students decide what they want to learn about, create, invent, make or figure out, and then they formulate a plan to do so. All of these steps take creativity and allow students to further practice creativity.

Some students may think they aren't creative. Well, if they weren't literate we wouldn't just say they can't read, but rather we would spend time

Figure 4.5 International Society for Technology in Education Standards for Students

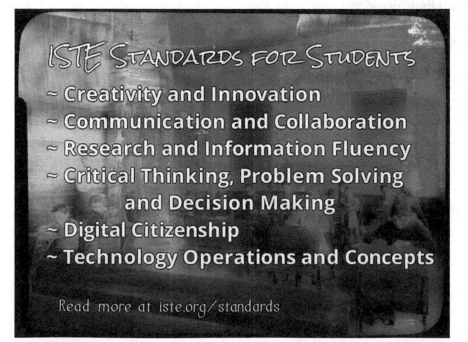

with them and have them practice and practice and practice; similarly, if our students claim not to be creative, then we need to give them time to practice. Genius Hour is one way to do that.

Communication and Collaboration

Both of us allow our students to work in groups for Genius Hour; this gives them an authentic way to collaborate on a project that they designed and that they are excited about. Not only can they work with classmates, but they can and do communicate and collaborate with people outside our classroom—experts and other classrooms around the world, for instance.

As we mentioned earlier, both of us have our students share their learning when they are done with their Genius Hour projects. What better way to practice our communication skills than to share the things we are most excited about? Not only can Genius Hour presentations be shared with fellow classmates, but parents, administration and other stakeholders can be invited as well. Some Genius Hour presentations are even live streamed for parents who can't be there, shared with another class live on Skype or recorded for uploading to YouTube.

Research and Information Fluency

Of course we should spend other academic time teaching research skills and how to properly curate information, but Genius Hour provides students with a fun way to practice these skills they are learning.

More and more, it is becoming important to teach students how to navigate through the abundance of information that they come across when they Google a topic. Memorizing facts becomes less important, and knowing how to tell what is accurate becomes more important. We encourage you to teach these skills and learning processes and allow Genius Hour to be a time for students to practice and for you, the teacher, to monitor the transfer of these skills. You read about the use of one valuable research tool—a KWHLAQ chart—in Chapter 3.

Critical Thinking, Problem Solving and Decision Making

In Genius Hour sessions, you will find that students definitely get an opportunity to think critically, make important decisions for the direction of the projects and constantly solve project problems. Initially, we noticed that many of our students came to us when they got stuck, but as time went on, students became more independent and tried to problem solve on their own first.

Another thing we noticed was that, because of the presentations, students learned more about each other and started to recognize each other's unique talents and skills. As a result, they began to seek each other out for help when they got stuck, before reaching out to the teacher. Students problem solving on their own and respecting their fellow students' knowledge? Sounds good to us!

Digital Citizenship

Because we both had our students blog about their Genius Hour projects, our students most definitely got time to work on their digital citizenship as a result of Genius Hour. And again, we cannot stress enough how significant it was for our students to share things that were meaningful to them. Genius Hour provided them with the content, motivation and time to share their learning, practice literacy and understand digital citizenship in an authentic way.

Many educators are calling for "digital citizenship" to be replaced with "citizenship," noting that as technology becomes ubiquitous it is important to be good citizens in regards to everything we do, and that perhaps it is no longer relevant to separate digital from non-digital citizenship. If we take this term and apply it in this broader way, students get to grow in the area of citizenship in countless ways during Genius Hour.

Technology Operations and Concepts

Most of our students use technology as part of their inquiry (things like laptops with Internet access, iPads, video cameras, etc.) while pursuing questions like: How does green screen technology work? How do you put special effects into a movie? What are the steps involved in stop motion? If not during their actual inquiry, then they used the technology as a way to share what they learned (slideshows, documentaries, websites, etc.). Because of this, we found that our students became more skilled in their ability to utilize and understand different technologies. Before Genius Hour, our middle-school students hadn't had the opportunity to learn programming, but as a result of letting them loose to learn like this, they began to create apps and learn programs such as Scratch and LEGO Mindstorms.

Use Technology as Available, When Needed

Many teachers ask us if they have to have access to technology in order to do Genius Hour, and the answer is not as easy as yes or no. Some students

Bring Your Own Device in action

Minecraft during Genius Hour

Student working on LEGO stop motion animation

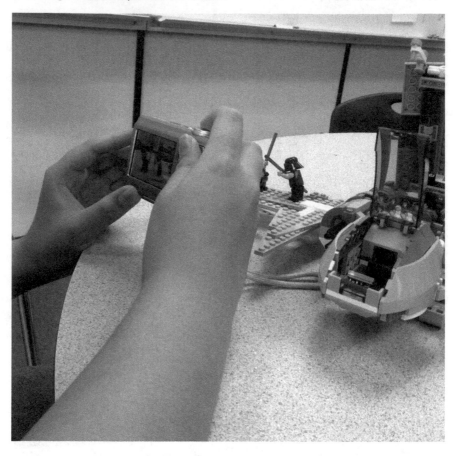

are comparing art mediums, or writing plays—these students do not really need tech in order to do their projects, but a lot of our students come up with research-based questions, and so having access to technology is important to these students.

If your school has access to a cart of laptops, iPads or other devices, you may want to plan your Genius Hour time for this block (or, even better, share with a colleague since you likely will not need access to all of the equipment on the cart; if you share, then you can both do Genius Hour and both have enough tech).

For the most part, students just use the technology that is available to them. Gallit was pleasantly surprised when she began implementing a BYOD program in her classroom. She had students bring in their own iPod touches, iPads and other tablets. About half of her students brought in their own devices, and then they had more than enough tech with all of that, in addition to their three classroom computers. (Students had to fill out some legal paperwork first.[2]) This makes it possible for all students to have access to the tools that they need, and they get good at asking for what they need too. When some of her students realized they needed lights to shine on the green screen for it to work properly, they approached the principal and asked him if they could borrow the theater lights from the gym. (This may not be a learning outcome for any given subject area, but figuring out your needs, having the courage to articulate your needs and asking for resources from the principal in a polite manner seems like all kinds of skills and learning happening!)

That being said, not every Genius Hour project is going to need access to technology. We have had students create new sports, compare art mediums, write stories and even bake. A lot of students choose to use technology in some sort of way during their Genius Hour (i.e. Internet for research, iMovie for documentary, camera for stop motion, etc.) but it is certainly not required. Students dream up their own projects. In fact, on one of Gallit's visits to neighboring schools, she came across one inquiry project that she will never forget. It was an urban garden project created by some high school students[3] at the Inquiry Hub School in Coquitlam, BC. If a student's passion is gardening, then that is what they should be doing for Genius Hour.

Baking is always a favorite Genius Hour activity, and the presentation is always a hit

Summary

Presentations are an exciting part of the Genius Hour process. Students love sharing their new areas of genius with the rest of their class and Genius Hour connects wonderfully to the ISTE standards and to many areas of our curriculum. In presentations, students practice literacy standards of speaking, listening, reading and writing. Genius Hour gives students an authentic opportunity to use those twenty-first-century learning skills that we all know are so important for today's learners to develop.

Notes

1 http://tinyurl.com/GHSmith
2 There are lots of examples of this if you search online. You can also check out Hugh's blog and links at http://tinyurl.com/GHbyod. You may also want to check with your School District or IT department to see if they have a BYOD policy in place.
3 You can follow the students at twitter.com/greeninquiry.

5

Helping Kids Make Their Learning Visible

Children must be taught how to think, not what to think.

Margaret Mead

We love seeing kids get curious about things, so in Genius Hour we begin with wonder. Next, we learn. We want kids to spend time learning about their wonders (be it through research, experimentation, invention, etc.). And lastly, *we share*. We want our students to share their new knowledge, creation, innovation.

We have talked about sharing through presentations to our classmates/school/parents, but what about the rest of the world? We want our students to make their learning visible, to share with the world!

Giving students an opportunity in school to make their learning visible is very powerful and a key part of Genius Hour learning. Students are asked to contribute to the world and, as Angela Maiers says, their contributions are needed and expected. Moreover, our students *want* to share because they are excited and passionate about the content. Sharing is also a great way for them to reinforce and reflect on their learning.

Use Blogs So Students Can Share with an Authentic Audience

When children create for the world, they make it good.

When children create only for their teacher, they make it good enough.

Rushton Hurley

For us and our students, blogging (and the next step, ePortfolios) has become an excellent vehicle for sharing and building community. Moreover, it is an authentic way to practice writing and online publishing. Genius Hour has given students exciting and genuine ideas for blogging. It is one thing to write something or produce something when you know that only your teacher will be looking at it, but it is a complete other thing to work on something that you know will be online, available for all of your friends, family and the world to see.

Many user-friendly blogging platforms are available to teachers (like Kidblog,[1] Edublogs[2] and Weebly[3]) and this gives our students a real audience with which to share their learning. They are so excited to learn that students in another classroom (down the hall or across the globe) have read and learned from their personal blogs. Of course, they also love the comments and questions they receive from their own classmates too! We give

Blogging about her favorite artists

class time to students to comment on each other's Genius Hour blog posts as a way to give and consider peer feedback. To easily share individual blog posts with your school community or a wider audience, make one post on a class blog and add links to individual or group Genius Hour presentations.[4]

Another delightful side-effect of children connecting with others around the world through blogging is that it allows children to be accepted in a new way. The bullies and the bullied, the straight-As and the strugglers, the cool and the nerdy, the introverted and extroverted, the acne-ed and the brace-faced, the very thin and the very round—it doesn't matter what we look like or how we are perceived on our campuses. Online we can all have a fresh start. We can all be on a level playing field. We can all make valuable contributions. Even the weakest students can do the work of the twenty-first century when they share their own genius. On their blogs, children have success sharing creations through video, music, art and other graphic media. In addition, weak writers strive to become better writers because they know an authentic audience is reading.

Read about the pedagogy of blogging on the Langwitches website.[5] And Denise wrote a blog post[6] just for you about how you, as a teacher, can better manage all your students' blog posts with a simple Google form.

Bring Traffic to the Blogs!

So, how can you get visitors to your students' blogs? Well, that is where you become the facilitator again! Find ways for them to connect with other classes. Remember having pen pals when you were younger? There are tons of Genius Hour classrooms that you can connect with. Kidblog.org has a great way for you to share only with selected other Kidblog classes if privacy is a concern. Alternatively, you can open it up to everyone, like we do, and share your link with classes that participate in the Global Genius Hour Project[7] created by Robyn Thiessen.

How about sharing the link with your principal and fellow teachers? Students love getting comments from principals, and what a great way to showcase what you are doing in the classroom with your administrator and school board. Encourage students to share their blogs with extended family members who live abroad. Gallit loved hearing from one student how their relative in India checked their blog regularly—it warms our hearts.

You can also use the hashtag #comments4kids, created by William Chamberlain, where educators post links of student work that deserves some extra comments. And while you are visiting the hashtag to post some of your student work, don't forget to pay it forward and comment on a few yourself.

Another great idea is to recruit some of your friends to make comments—especially if any of them work in a field a student is passionate about. Find connections and mentors for your class!

Blogging has become our favorite way to share student work. It is a foundational skill to teach children. A blog is a place to which all other digital publications can be linked or embedded to share with a broader audience.

Teacher Tip: What If I Don't Use Student Blogs in My Class?

Well, may we start by suggesting that you should consider blogging with your class? It is very simple to set up and there are plenty of free options. Gallit likes kidblog.org because it is made for teachers and students and it has different levels of security (you can have it set to public, private or semi-private). Denise's favorite is edublogs.org because the support team has gone above and beyond to help her and her students become bloggers.

An excellent idea for those who aren't yet ready for children to start their own blogs is a class blog where the teacher posts and the students are limited to just commenting. If they have made online presentations, you can add links to other media or photos to a blog post. You can also begin to identify those individuals who are ready to write blog posts on behalf of the class.

If blogging is not yet a possibility, then what about starting with a paper blog? We have seen teachers use paper-blogging formats in their classrooms. Students write up a reflection on cute paper with a computer screen border and then, in a gallery walk format, students spend some time walking around the room and commenting on the paper-blogs with post-it note comments. That way, your class can still receive peer feedback.

Consider ePortfolios for Collections of Work

Another way students can share their learning is through an ePortfolio. This can be done in a few different ways, through a student-created website or through a program like FreshGrade where both students and teachers can upload information that communicates what the students are learning. Gallit used Weebly with her students, and they created ePortfolios on their own personal websites. Students had a page for each subject (including Genius Hour) and they posted pictures of their work, descriptions and reflections on what they learned. Students loved working on their ePortfolios.

Don't Forget Other Online Sharing Options

Hugh McDonald helps students share their learning in a variety of ways. "They share via in-class presentations, their blog/e-Portfolio, my YouTube account, and via our classroom Twitter account." As Hugh says, blogging isn't the only way to make learning visible. Besides his examples of posting on YouTube and Twitter, some other options you might consider for online publishing include Vimeo, Instagram, Flickr, Glogster, Storybird, Facebook, Scribd, Google Slides, Documents, Drawings and Sites, Slideshare, Tackk, ThingLink, MoveNote and so much more. Check out this post[8] of forty-four tools to publish your students' work. Anything your student creates online will have an embed code or a link that they can share with friends and stakeholders. If you want to wait on blogging, find one or two online tools that you and your students enjoy and find useful. Then share your learning with the world using those publications.

Summary

We believe that sharing our learning is a key step in the learning process. We were both amazed at how seriously our students took their work when they knew it would be shared online, and how game-changing it is when you finally have guests comment on your work. It is also a wonderful way for students to contribute to the world. Blogging, ePortfolios and other online publications help the teacher and student keep track of their learning and provide engaging ways for students to give and receive peer feedback.

Notes

1 http://kidblog.org/home
2 http://edublogs.org
3 http://www.weebly.com
4 Example: http://tinyurl.com/GHBlogIndex
5 http://tinyurl.com/BlogPedagogy
6 http://tinyurl.com/BlogPostForm
7 http://tinyurl.com/globalGH
8 http://tinyurl.com/44techtools

6

Teaching about
Self-Assessment and Feedback

The illiterate of the 21st century will not be those who cannot read and write, but those who cannot learn, unlearn and relearn.

Alvin Toffler

How do you assess Genius Hour? Well, everything worth doing is worth assessing and reflecting on, so we need to consider the importance of formative and self-assessment in Genius Hour. How do we arrange for our students to give and receive feedback that moves them forward into their future learning? (See Figure 6.1 for a handy feedback infographic.) If assessment is going to happen honestly and safely, we feel that grading should not be part of Genius Hour learning.

We are giving over instructional decisions to the children. They are given autonomy, choose the purpose and can take the time needed for mastery. The children can also help decide how they want to grow through the experience. Teachers, though, have an important part in teaching students about assessing themselves and accepting constructive feedback from others. Possible areas for assessment are creativity, digital citizenship, research and literacy skills, presentation techniques and twenty-first-century skills like collaboration, problem solving and others you will have read about in Chapter 4. Let's look at how you can teach students to assess themselves in these areas.

Figure 6.1 Feedback that Feeds Forward

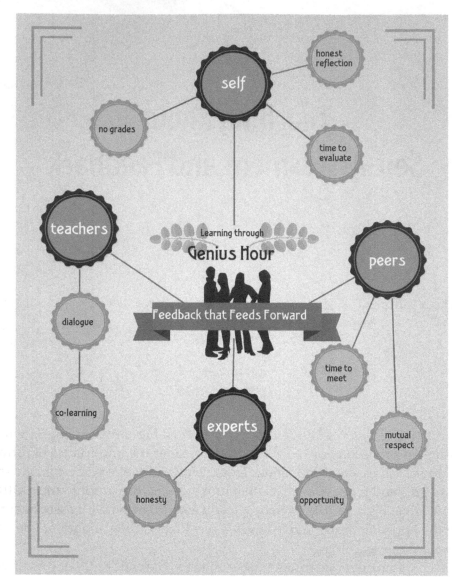

Source: http://tinyurl.com/GHFeedForward

Use Self-Assessment Rubrics and Question Starters

As a teacher, you can give students valuable time to reflect on their learning. One area that we feel strongly about is having our students grow in "creativity." What steps do we take throughout Genius Hour that allow them to see that they are moving forward? How do they assess creativity for themselves and make sure they are headed in the right direction? We want our young children to grow up to be creative thinkers and problem solvers, who are ready for future workplaces of innovation. If they are not actively learning and positively practicing creativity, they will lose it. Genius Hour is a way to nurture the entrepreneurial spirit in young people.

We ask students to assess their own growth in qualities of creativity and innovation, such as willingness to live with ambiguity, inquisitiveness, idea generation, originality, flexibility, self-reflection, intrinsic motivation, risk taking, expertise and persistence. Students can complete the Self-Assessment of Creativity Traits rubric two or three times a year to see how they are growing in understanding and practicing these traits. (This self-assessment can be found in Appendix B.)

It is worth noting that if you haven't done a lot of self-assessment, and quite frankly even if you have, you ought to spend some time with your students teaching them how to self-assess. The first time that Gallit gave her students the self-assessment, she found that a lot of students were too critical of themselves, or, on the flip side, a lot of students gave themselves 5/5 on areas that they probably still needed to work on . . . a lot. Besides teaching the group the basics, one-on-one conferences with students will help them. Self-assessment is so important, as is learning how to use a rubric and set goals for oneself, so this is definitely worth exploring with your students.

Remember when you were in teacher education and you had to write reflections? We know that reflection is important and so, besides having students self-assess with rubrics, we also encourage them to write reflections during Genius Hour. This can be done using journals or on their blogs. We used to do this periodically, but Robyn Thiessen likes to end each Genius Hour session with a self-reflection blog entry. Students answer four questions:

1. What did I do?
2. What did I learn?
3. What was successful? What failed?
4. What is next?

We think Robyn's weekly Genius Hour reflections are a great idea! As John Dewey said, "We do not learn from experience, we learn from reflecting on experience."

More Self-Assessment Questions for Students

During the Project Process

◆ Looking at my work so far, how can I keep focusing on answering my inquiry question?

◆ What have I done well so far?

◆ What do I need to do to move forward? (Gather supplies? Ask a friend or teacher to help me evaluate the next step? Revise my inquiry question?)

◆ What will completion of my project look like? How can I take the next step toward completing it?

Research Checklist

◆ When I learn something new from a web page or book, do I make a note of where I got my information so I can cite my sources?

◆ Am I careful not to plagiarize? Do I read and learn from my sources and then close the book or web page and tell or write what I learned?

After Presentation

◆ Was my voice loud enough for all to hear? Did I speak slowly enough and enunciate so I could be understood?

◆ Did I make eye contact with my audience? (Or do I need to practice not reading my notes or presentation slides?)

◆ What was one way I communicated well to show what I learned?

◆ What is one way I can better communicate my learning the next time I present Genius Hour?

Allow Time to Practice Peer Feedback

As discussed in the previous chapter, we like to ensure that our students are writing and sharing about their learning journey and that peers have the opportunity to comment and ask questions of one another on their blog posts.

Peer feedback does not come easily to all learners, and so it may be beneficial to spend some time talking about what constructive feedback looks like, modeling and perhaps setting up some feedback criteria. Use "Pair and Share" for students to discuss and explain their work to a partner. Partners should be specific in saying what went well and how their partner's learning is progressing. Then partners can offer at least one piece of advice that their friend can take to make it even better, to move their learning forward.

All learners should be able to give and receive respectful peer feedback. However, it will take practice. The teacher must teach and model and gradually release responsibility to students. You don't want to just pair students up and have them talk about their projects. Create or adopt some common classroom vocabulary or acronyms to help with peer assessment. Then be consistent with how that vocabulary is defined. For instance, you instruct the children, "Tell your partner *what went well*." If you have taught and practiced with students that *what went well* means to tell at least one specific thing that was good—information that is related to the learning—then they won't answer, "I like it" or "It's cool." They will have learned to say something like, "The words on your poster are big and easy to read. The dark letters on the light background will be read even from the back of the room. And everything is spelled right."

After students learn how, the teacher should make time in the day to allow students to get together to learn from each other. This can happen before, during or after Genius Hour. Time spent learning how to give and receive peer feedback will certainly help them in all areas, not just Genius Hour.

Peer Feedback Questions

◆ What went well?
◆ What can I do to make it better?
◆ What more do you wish you could learn about my topic? What's missing?
◆ What else can you tell me so I can be successful?

Give Students the Chance to Receive Expert Feedback

Experts are busy with their own important work in the field, and who knows better what your Genius Hour students are learning than those who are working it daily? Children who are serious about their work should seek out the opportunity to receive feedback from experts in the field. We think of Jack Andraka,[1] who through research and collaboration with Anirban Maitra, an expert at Johns Hopkins University, developed an early-detection test for pancreatic cancer.

Today children are able to connect with experts in their field of study through emails, Twitter, Facebook and other social media applications. Social media has made it very easy to connect with experts. In fact, beware of this ease, for it is too easy for a child or teacher to write a flippant tweet or email. Children should be encouraged to contact experts only after diligent work on their part. We might mention that Jack had already worked diligently and was sure of his work when he sought expert help to be able to use the lab at Johns Hopkins. Besides the one affirmative response, he also received 199 rejection emails from other experts at Johns Hopkins.

We do not wish to discourage the use of experts. On the contrary, honest feedback from an expert in photography, engineering, baking, language study, aviation or whatever field your student is interested in will go further than much teacher feedback. We also want to acknowledge that you don't need to find experts only at high-profile institutions like Johns Hopkins University. There are many adults and retirees in our communities who are anxious to share their knowledge and help children. We hope you will help your students reach out to experts and mentors appropriately, guiding them to respectfully make connections to receive valuable feedback.

Make Sure Your Own Feedback Is a Meaningful Dialogue

> This is at the heart of all good education, where the teacher asks students to think and engages them in encouraging dialogues, constantly checking for understanding and growth.
>
> William Glasser

Meaningful feedback from teachers happens in dialogue—not as an authority figure speaking down to the student. This kind of dialogue between teacher and student looks more like vibrant, enthusiastic conversation, connecting co-learners and collaborators. These interactions with our students have transformed the learning culture in our classrooms. Over the last three years, as teachers we have enthusiastically said, in ways that we had not in our previous years of teaching, things like, "How did you do that?", "Do it again!", "Show me what you did!" We have embraced a dialogue approach to feedback and feed-forward: "What are you going to try next?"

As teachers, during Genius Hour, we formatively assess students during casual observation and in one-to-one dialogues or small-group discussions.

There are many skill areas that are practiced and mastered during Genius Hour—technology, researching, reading, writing, listening, speaking, presenting. Teachers find that Genius Hour projects often cover many state/provincial content and prescribed learning outcomes. When we see that children are practicing and mastering these skills, we certainly take time to give them credit for the skills, whether on a checklist, standards-based report card, narrative feedback documentation or through some other method of recording students meeting the standards.

Common Core Standards Met Through Genius Hour

Here are just four of the Common Core Standards for a variety of grade levels. These and *most* other standards in the Common Core can be practiced during Genius Hour.

CCSS.ELA-LITERACY.RI.4.3

Explain events, procedures, ideas or concepts in a historical, scientific or technical text, including what happened and why, based on specific information in the text.

CCSS.ELA-LITERACY.SL.5.4

Report on a topic or text or present an opinion, sequencing ideas logically and using appropriate facts and relevant, descriptive details to support main ideas or themes; speak clearly at an understandable pace.

CCSS.ELA-LITERACY.RST.6-8.7

Integrate quantitative or technical information expressed in words in a text with a version of that information expressed visually (e.g., in a flowchart, diagram, model, graph or table).

CCSS.ELA-LITERACY.RH.6-8.7

Integrate visual information (e.g., in charts, graphs, photographs, videos or maps) with other information in print and digital texts.

British Columbia's Prescribed Learning Outcomes

The following can be practiced in Genius Hour:

Grade 4 English Language Arts – Oral Language

A9. Use speaking and listening to improve and extend thinking, by:

- acquiring new ideas;
- making connections and asking questions;
- comparing and analyzing ideas;
- developing explanations;
- considering alternative viewpoints;
- investigating problems and creating solutions.

The BC curriculum is undergoing significant revision right now and the new draft curriculum has even more connections to Genius Hour, especially within the three core competencies:

Communication

"The communication competency encompasses the set of abilities that students use to impart and exchange information, experiences and ideas, to explore the world around them, and to understand and effectively engage in the use of digital media."

Creative Thinking

"The thinking competency encompasses the knowledge, skills and processes we associate with intellectual development. It is through their competency as thinkers that students take subject-specific concepts and content and transform them into a new understanding. Thinking competence includes specific thinking skills as well as habits of mind, and metacognitive awareness."

Personal and Social

"Personal and social competency is the set of abilities that relate to students' identity in the world, both as individuals and as members of their community and society. Personal and social competency encompasses the abilities students need to thrive as individuals, to understand and care about themselves and others, and to find and achieve their purposes in the world."[2]

Students are proving mastery of these and many other learning outcomes all over British Columbia as they participate in Genius Hour.

Assess but Don't Grade

We are all for assessing Genius Hour. Grading is a different issue, though. We agree that Genius Hour projects should be left ungraded. We agree with Hugh McDonald when he says students learn for love and passion rather than grades. See Figure 6.2.

We believe in assessment *for* learning. Students do not need assessment *of* learning for these passion projects. Genius Hour projects should not be marked with a grade of A, B, C, etc. and added to a gradebook. Genius Hour should be a safe time to really learn.

Teachers are wise when they let students have at least some autonomy away from the burden of marks on a report card. Students will learn. You will have the opportunity to see, perhaps for the first time, what true learning, creating and producing look like away from the threat or reward of a report card.

Imagine for a moment receiving a mark or percentage on the passion projects that you choose. Pretend that you are going to try baking or guitar playing for the first time.

◆ Grades on baking cookies: "They were too hard, so I'll give you an 80%."

Figure 6.2 Tweet by Hugh McDonald

Hugh McDonald
@hughtheteacher

☼ Following

A7: Premise behind #geniushour is the motivation behind their why for doing it... love and passion over grades #CAedchat

↩ Reply ↻ Retweeted ★ Favorite ••• More

Source: https://twitter.com/hughtheteacher/status/333791599106613249

No. Instead, how about if the consumers of the cookies just enjoy them dunked in milk or coffee? Or, if you have a mentor baker, he might suggest that you turn these dry cookies into a delicious trifle. Or he could teach you to try again and take them out of the oven a minute or two before they are finished because they continue to bake when taken out of the oven.

◆ Grades on learning to play the guitar as an adult: "Oh, it was pretty good, but your guitar was not quite in tune on that Beatles song and you missed that B flat chord a couple times, so I'll give you an 83%."

No. Instead of a grade, how about just enjoying the satisfaction of making music after all the previous years of not trying? Or, if you have a mentor musician, she might teach you how to use an electronic guitar tuner. A grade might discourage, rather than encourage, you to keep trying to get that B flat right.

Both the cookies and guitar playing are examples of passion projects one of us might choose to do. We all have passion projects of our own, and whatever yours is, you certainly understand how much more valuable helpful feedback and feed-forward are than getting a percentage marked on your passion products!

The same goes with children. Children will choose their learning based on their passions for Genius Hour. How devastating if they have to be evaluated and given a grade for their passionate efforts. We must create that safe place to practice many standards, including ISTE's twenty-first-century skills of creativity and innovation; communication and collaboration; research and information fluency; critical thinking, problem solving and decision making; digital citizenship; and technology operations and concepts—skills that are hard to systematize and quantify in our grading systems. If you watch closely, you will notice students demonstrating mastery of many skills and exhibiting deep understanding of concepts in the curriculum. Of course, they should receive credit for mastering skills and understanding these concepts. This will especially make sense if you use standards-based grading. However, we believe that having strict rubrics and teacher evaluation of the projects should be avoided.

We know that some folks will be worried about students not taking their project seriously if there are no grades. However, we would encourage you to give them a chance, and we think they will take it seriously. In fact, Genius Hour teachers all over the world know from personal experience that they will. We believe students work hard because they love what they are doing. They have the autonomy to choose their own project and that autonomy

Figure 6.3 100% against the way we traditionally do grades

and purpose are what keep them motivated. Sure, we have had students ask about letter grades and marks when it comes to Genius Hour, but that can be turned into a teachable moment conversation about a growth mindset, work ethic and the difference between intrinsic and extrinsic motivation.

Over the past several years, Gallit has tried to get her students to move away from questions like "How many marks is this worth?" to questions like "What part of my work needs improvement to get it to be great?" By focusing on formative assessment, students can learn to improve their work, rather than just being handed a summative grade/mark. This is not always an easy transition for students—it will take time for some of your students.

Need more info on this? If you haven't already seen it, we suggest you watch Daniel Pink in his TED Talk[3] about motivation.

Summary

Students participating in Genius Hour should self-assess. They should also receive the benefit of helpful feedback from peers, experts and teachers to push their learning to the next level. Genius Hour works best with Assessment for Learning (formative assessment) practices. We don't grade Genius Hour projects; it is a time for students and teachers to practice and enjoy learning. If you must, you can leave the grading (and summative assessment practices) for the other subjects. (But as the cartoon in Figure 6.3 illustrates, you might want to reconsider *all* letter and percentage grading.)

Notes

1 http://tinyurl.com/TEDJack
2 https://curriculum.gov.bc.ca/competencies
3 http://tinyurl.com/TEDmotivation

7

What Can We Do to Improve the World?

Education is the most powerful weapon we can use to change the world.

Nelson Mandela

"You are a genius, and the world needs your contribution," says Angela Maiers. You might be thinking, "Me? The world needs me?"

Four years ago, when Denise began her journey as a connected educator, one of the ways she contributed was by adding photos to her Flickr Photostream.[1] Other people used the photos for blog posts, calendars, even as cover art for a campy vampire book. Sometimes she added quotes about learning and change and shared them with other teachers. This simple act of contributing, and others that people do every day, improve the world. It makes the world smaller, more friendly and collaborative. It adds good content to the Internet, making it an even better place.

In Genius Hour, students give art to the world, share recipes, create websites, teach a craft, make music and produce films. When students create and produce, and then share their learning beyond the classroom walls, it contributes to the good of the world. Genius Hour helps us become producers and makers, not just consumers.

In their newfound empowerment, students and classes will begin to take on bigger challenges. They will start to answer the questions Angela Maiers asks of geniuses: "What breaks your heart about the world? How will you act on it?"

How Denise Challenged Her Students to Make a Difference

One year, Denise was having a difficult time getting students to "Scale up Genius Hour."[2] She had given plenty of pep talks, but she didn't feel the Genius Hour projects were reaching the potential her students had. However, one spring day, unintentionally, students accepted the challenge to take action. It was in using the KWHLAQ chart, described in Chapter 3, that students got thinking about how they could make a difference.

Denise's experience, shared in a blog post written the next day ("Such a Simple Question: What Action Will I Take?"[3]), is reprinted below.

Inspiring Students to Act

Last night during our Genius Hour Twitter chat and book study of Angela Maiers and Amy Sanvold's *The Passion-Driven Classroom*, I was inspired by passionate educators who inspire passion in their students. I wondered how to help young teens harness their energetic spirit and begin to use it to make the world a better place.

How do I inspire them to act? Could they ever be ready for Angela's Quest2Matter?

Well, little did I know that I would come to school today, and they would be thinking the same thing I was. How did that happen?

I do have an idea about what inspired them, and it's very simple. And unrelated to my pep talks.

In science, they were working on a researcher's workshop project on something related to genetics, DNA or heredity. After watching a recent video interview with Paul Solarz, I had decided to try the KWHLAQ [Figure 7.1] he had learned about from Silvia Rosenthal Tolisano on her Langwitches.com site. (Awesome resources coming from these great connections!)

Well, when they got to the "A" column—"What action will I take?"—they took the chart seriously. They didn't even ask me questions about it. They just started brainstorming. Five of them had chosen to study some aspect of Down syndrome, and they were working on the same Google Document. I started hearing things like, "Let's go on a Buddy Walk," "Let's have a car wash and raise money for GiGi's Playhouse" and "Let's play games with the residents at Hope Haven."

Figure 7.1 KWHLAQ chart

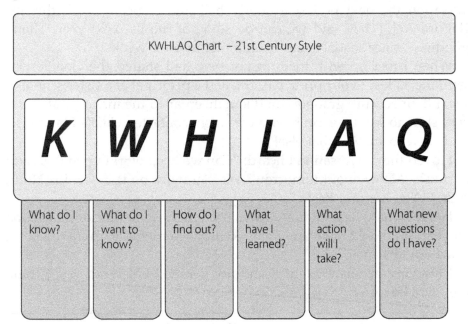

Source: Used with permission of Silvia Rosenthal Tolisano (@Langwitches); www.flickr.com/photos/langwitches/5958295132

Figure 7.2 A look at their Google Doc with their "ACTION" ideas

Down Syndrome Ideas:

- Car wash with lemonade and cookies on May 21, 9–1:30, Hyvee parking lot Sioux city
- Buddy walk
- Sweet corn

JDRF Ideas:

- Walk for the cure
- Prick yourself

Hunger Ideas:

- 30-hour famine
- Soup kitchen

They didn't stop with Down syndrome. They continued their conversation the next period in study hall and came up with this list [Figure 7.2]. (They said we can do some of the list next year. Thank goodness, since school is out for summer in three weeks!)

When I met up with them again, they had shared the Google Doc with me, talked to our principal, emailed a principal at a sister school to see if their seventh graders could join in, emailed the manager at a grocery store to see if we can have a car wash, contacted GiGi's Playhouse, and . . . who knows what else!

I loved the conversation I heard: "Can we keep working on this sixth period?", "How about tomorrow? We can work on it in Genius Hour, right?" Yes, Yes and Yes!

Here, I would have thought I was trying to inspire this kind of action all year. If I would have known, I would have tried the upgraded KWL chart months ago!

I love my genius students! And my genius PLN! And, yes, I think they will be ready!

This student and her partner made scarves to sell at a benefit for her classmate's family

Ways to Help Students Take on Bigger Issues and Affect Change

The questions "What breaks your heart about the world?" and "How will you act on it?" have children answer the call to make a difference in the lives of people within our world (see the photo on the previous page for a Genius Hour project focused on making a difference)—modern slavery, illiteracy, poverty, cancer and homelessness, just to start. Get your students thinking about those questions by leading them through "heartbreak" mapping. In Angela Maier's article, "Forget Following Your Heart, Follow Your HeartBreak,"[4] Karen McMillan suggests having children and youth brainstorm on three tiers to map their hearts and heartbreaks—in the center, what are you passionate about?; on the second tier, what breaks your heart about those things?; finally, on the outside, what are ideas to ease those heartbreaks?

Oliver Schinkten (@schink10) calls his hybrid of passion-based learning and Genius Hour "Com-passion based learning." His website describes it as "empowering students to make a positive contribution to the community through their passion."[5] Oliver is a compassionate educator, helping lead others to educational transformation.

As Angela also says, "Kids don't want to be needy, they want to be needed." They want to make a difference. In fact, children are our role models in standing up against injustice . . . if we would just let them. Students will lead adults as they work for the benefit of others with their engagement and energy. You can join Angela's global movement called Choose2Matter[6] for more ways that your students can make a difference.

Watching Your Students Change the World Will Change the Entire Way You Teach

Genius Hour will be a catalyst for big changes in the teacher and classroom too. Everything changed for us. More choices throughout the school day become inevitable. Here is a comment and response from a Genius Hour blog post by Lisa Nowakowski:[7]

COMMENT: Lisa – Great post. I'm so glad you're doing Genius Hour with the kiddos! It really changes the entire way you teach.

REPLY: It does change the way I teach. I learned pretty early on to stay out of the way. It really is my favorite part of the week too. The students are engaged the entire hour. It's awesome.

Teachers all over the world are saying the same thing!

When we took seriously what motivates people—autonomy, mastery, purpose—we began to give students 1.5–2 hours a week to learn what they wanted to. Those Genius "Hour" times were precious to us all—students and teachers—but so much more changed as well. During the rest of the week, we began to give students more choices—from where they sat in class, to whom they worked with, to how they showed mastery of the standards they needed to learn.

The Genius Hour inquiry process inspired us to use more inquiry-based learning in other subject areas too. Denise began to ask students what they wanted to learn in history and science. Why not? The Common Core Standards no longer dictate the traditional eighth-grade American history curriculum, which was prehistoric North America to Reconstruction. Now students are able to meet the standards by applying the learnings to various eras in our history. There are similar changes happening (or already in place) in various provinces in Canada too.

Committed as they drill a hole in the water trough

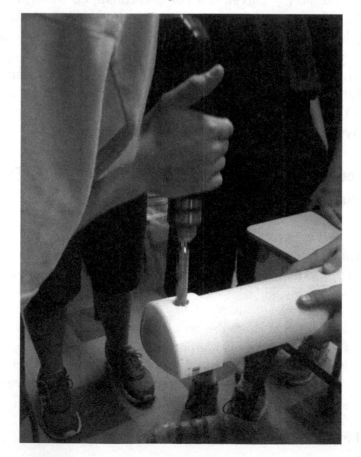

We also began to give children more time. Before we learned this process, we often found children did not have enough time to master what we asked them to learn. We've become more appreciative of the process of learning and motivation. Learning takes time. When students have a passion about something, they want to do it. *A lot*. Why don't we let them?

The water trough shown below, needed for a unit in science class, was hard to empty and often got tipped over, spilling water in the classroom. Students saw a need, and because of the changes in their learning environment—because of Genius Hour—Denise trusted them to fix it. The first thing they did was drill a hole into our trough! They were brave engineers, as you'll see in the following photo.

After drilling a drain hole, they added a hose and faucet and built a stand to raise it up. They did most of this work at home and during recess. They brought their own supplies. They received no grade and no school credit, just the joy of creating and producing and helping our classroom. The new-and-improved trough now withstands upsets, is easily drained and, best of all, is perfectly theirs. The photo below shows the finished product.

As another example, in Gallit's class, her students had been doing Genius Hour for quite a few months (some for more than a year as she looped many students) and students were beginning to make that switch from projects of

Finishing up solving the water trough problem

personal interest to projects that make a difference in the world. And then in the week leading up to Valentine's Day, students decided they wanted to start doing random acts of kindness for the entire school—they called themselves the Kindness Ninjas and, even though it was meant to last until Valentine's Day, the Kindness Ninjas were known to pull off anonymous random acts of kindness all year long (anonymous until now—I guess we just revealed their secret identities . . . Oops!).

Choice, trust, engagement and true learning—these are all by-products that happen in our classrooms as a result of Genius Hour.

If your classroom is fully teacher-centered and you just experiment with Genius Hour, with no other changes, Genius Hour may not be successful. You may try it, but you'll probably abandon it, saying it doesn't work with "my students," or some other excuse.

As we said, *everything* begins to change when you start Genius Hour. More trust, more choice, more connections, more learning. It has to. Genius Hour is just part of the picture. Are you already open to more transformation in your classroom? Perhaps you can introduce even more personalized learning. Nichole Carter, eighth-grade ELA teacher from Portland, Oregon, describes on her Edutopia post[8] how Genius Hour plays a role in these six essentials of personalized learning:

1. Dual teacher role.
2. Learn about your students.
3. Create a culture of collaboration.
4. Create an interactive learning environment.
5. Build flexible pacing, but with structure.
6. Create authentic assessments.

For those of you who are ready for even more transformation in your classroom, you should read the book *ROLE Reversal* by Mark Barnes and consider jumping into a "results only learning environment," which is a lot like Genius Hour all day.

In addition, A.J. Juliani has recently started talking about "Genius Curriculum."[9] You can read his book *Inquiry and Innovation: Using 20% Time, Genius Hour and PBL to Drive Student Success* to take the next steps toward more project-based learning (PBL) in your curriculum.

Genius Hour Could Transform Students' Futures, Beyond School Doors

In *Who Owns the Learning: Preparing Students for Success in the Digital Age*, Alan November quotes William Cook (*Strategic Planning in America's Schools*,

1995) speaking in the last century about today: "Truly educated people in the next century will not apply for a job. They will create their own."

During Genius Hour, a student may study about Phineas Gage, "the man with a hole in his head," and grow up to discover advancements in neurology.

During Genius Hour, students can communicate with a pilot through email and Twitter and become inspired to take flying lessons as soon as they are old enough.

During Genius Hour, students may start building robots with LEGO Mindstorms and consider a career in programming or engineering.

In fact, one of Gallit's proudest days came when she received this tweet (see Figure 7.3) from the parent of a student. This student, N, now has a goal and dream for the future, all because he was allowed to take apart and put together computers as part of his Genius Hour project.

During Genius Hour, students become collaborators and creative, problem-solving thinkers, the ones in the twenty-first century that William Cook described. The ones who will create their own jobs. The people our world needs.

And once this starts to happen during Genius Hour, we know that it will start to spill into the rest of your week. Genius Hour is not an end in itself. We do not recommend teachers stop here, but only start here. For some teacher-centered educators, Genius Hour may be the first baby step in a transformation of what school can be for their students. For others, it is just another step on the journey they have already begun as lifelong learning, connected educators.

In fact, when we began Genius Hour, it wasn't as a way to make up for the rest of the "boring, teacher-centered" week. Our pedagogical visions were already starting to evolve and we were looking for ways to grow. Genius Hour was *a part of the journey*, not the entire thing. We think Genius Hour

Figure 7.3 Tweet by Susan Taylor

Susan Taylor
@Susan_Tayl0r
✿ +⚫ Follow

@gallit_z outcome of #GeniusHour learning - N says he is going to become an IT tech!

↩ ↻ ★ •••

FAVORITE
1

12:21 AM - 26 Feb 2013

Source: https://twitter.com/mydoulasue/status/306272812472102912

makes an excellent starting point if you are just beginning this journey or an excellent addition to your voyage if you have already begun to transform your teaching. You can find more in the FAQs (Appendix A) about how your whole school day is transformed.

Education isn't about what the teacher does; it's about what the child learns. Learning happens in every subject area when students are given autonomy, have purpose and are given time to master learning. They need time to create and produce. These opportunities need to find their way into 100% of the time we are with our students.

Summary

Children want to be needed. They need to be trusted to learn and to improve the world. Genius Hour gives them that opportunity and, before you know it, that passion and compassion will start to flow into all aspects of school. You never know where it will take you and your class and, indeed, your whole school. So is the next step improving the world? We believe that with Genius Hour, it just might be!

Notes

1 www.flickr.com/photos/mrsdkrebs
2 http://tinyurl.com/GHScaleUp
3 See the blog post for added links: http://tinyurl.com/GHAction
4 http://tinyurl.com/AngelaHeartbreak
5 http://tinyurl.com/GHSchinkten
6 http://choose2matter.org
7 http://lisanowakowski.com
8 http://tinyurl.com/GHCarter
9 http://tinyurl.com/GeniusCurriculum

8

Adding All Our Voices to the Genius Hour Movement

Self-education is, I firmly believe, the only kind of education there is.

Isaac Asimov

Thank you for making it to the end of our book! We hope you have begun to see why we both agree that Genius Hour was one of the best things we brought into our practice. It has been so amazing to see our students get really excited about learning, and in turn, this got us more excited about teaching. In fact, Genius Hour has impacted just about everything we do in the classroom. By implementing Genius Hour, we began to think critically about everything we were doing in our teaching practice. We began to ask ourselves how else we could engage our learners, and our overall pedagogy began to shift.

Teachers Share How Genius Hour Has Transformed Their Learning Environment

Our book just wouldn't be complete without another wonderful quote from our friend Joy Kirr, who agrees with us about the changes that follow Genius Hour. When we interviewed her about Genius Hour in her classroom, she revealed the following:

My students are so much more open with me—they ask me "Why?" and "Can I . . . ?" and "Couldn't we . . . ?" so much more than in prior years. And they hear "Why not?" much more from me than ever before. If something doesn't disrupt their learning and is safe (physically and mentally), I'm more likely to say "Why not?" to their requests than I ever was. In this way, however, they might not realize that they're doing much more work than I am—and they're learning more as a result.

We love the way implementing Genius Hour has changed so much in her classroom. Joy continued by explaining:

Some days I feel like I've made a complete turnaround. I give so much more choice than I have in prior years . . .

Students decorate the room. Many put up their own ideas made at home.

There is no teacher desk. It is converted into a student station, with supplies for students to use whenever they have a need. They no longer ask me for supplies, and some have even chosen to restock it for later. (They can also sit there!)

The only front of the room is when we have the projector on. The rest of the room is fair game for where the speaker (me or a student) stands. (I'm actually always on the move.)

Students can choose where (and how) to sit, as long as it's safe and not distracting to them or others. (We have a rocking chair, rolling chair, cushions, etc . . . some students sit on the floor or table as well.)

Students take pictures and choose the best of the day for our movie updates for parents.

Students can write in response to a prompt of their choice, as long as they write in relation to our goal or focus for the day.

Student passions are used as catalysts for discussions or writing, or reading, or . . . Students read what they choose and give book talks when they choose.

Students have blogs for authentic purposes—*not* for grades. Yes, it's true—some haven't chosen to write on them yet, but more have than last year.

I learn so much from them—how to organize the class, how to turn in assignments in different manners, how to move our tables for certain lessons, etc.

I'm much better at letting students know *why* we do things in class—and I'm better at making my lessons relevant to life, and not just ELA class.

Robyn Thiessen also feels like Genius Hour has changed her as an educator. When we asked her the question "Since starting Genius Hour, how have you changed as a teacher?" she replied:

> Before beginning Genius Hour in my classroom, I feel that I was a typical teacher, I thought that I was giving students ownership of their learning and choice. But GH has taught me to let go, to support rather than smother, to let my students fail, to let them have choice, to let them be noisy! I think that the best way to describe GH time in my room is . . . controlled chaos! It is the busiest, most invigorating time of the week! I am exhausted afterward! GH was the beginning of my transformation as an educator; seeing the success of student choice has pushed me to question other "standard" practices, such as assessment and reporting!

Similarly, Marianne Smith blogged:

> All of my students were engaged, all of my students were happy, all of my students were learning!! I was happy and I was learning . . . It was an unbelievable "AHA" moment. It truly was an awakening within myself and within my teaching practice.

Paul Solarz does Passion Time with his grade 5 students and he notes in his blog:

> It is a time for them to recharge, and a time for them to be selfish. It is a time for students to individualize their learning—they do what they want at their level of understanding. No one feels dumb during Passion Time. No one is bored during Passion Time.[1]

See Figures 8.1–8.5 for more tweets from teachers who have seen Genius Hour make a real difference.

Figure 8.1 Tweet by Keith Peters

Keith Peters
@principalkp

☼ Following

Beauty of #geniushour: provides Ss opportunity to create something that's intrinsically theirs rather than completing what is given to them.

↩ Reply ⇄ Retweet ★ Favorited ••• More

Source: https://twitter.com/principalkp/status/485860233240387584

Figure 8.2 Tweet by Katelyn Fraser

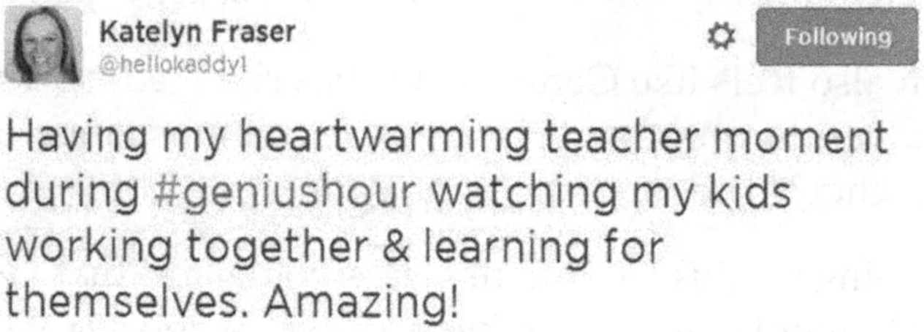

Katelyn Fraser
@hellokaddy1

☼ Following

Having my heartwarming teacher moment
during #geniushour watching my kids
working together & learning for
themselves. Amazing!

Source: https://twitter.com/hellokaddy1/status/499411895468560384

Figure 8.3 Tweet by Joy Kirr

Joy Kirr
@JoyKirr

☼ Following

I've never talked so much w/my students
until I started #geniushour. You really get
to know your children. #grateful

↶ Reply ⇄ Retweet ★ Favorite ••• More

Source: https://twitter.com/JoyKirr/statuses/352602384943423489

Figure 8.4 Tweet by Hugh McDonald

Hugh McDonald
@hughtheteacher

☼ Following

#geniushour looks messy & out of control
at 1st. But sit back. watch & listen
personalized, passionate, & engaged
learners in action. Magic!

↶ Reply ⇄ Retweet ★ Favorite ••• More

Source: https://twitter.com/hughtheteacher/statuses/352605613634764802

Figure 8.5 Tweet by Kay Bisaillon

Source: https://twitter.com/KayBisaillon/status/586861436858736641

And check out Figures 8.6–8.10 for advice for teachers that are new to Genius Hour. These were also shared on Twitter.

Figure 8.6 Tweet by Joel Pardalis

Source: https://twitter.com/MrPardalis/statuses/352604593080901632

Figure 8.7 Tweet by Joy Kirr

Joy Kirr
@JoyKirr

Jump in, ask students for help, follow your nose.
#geniushour
livebinders.com/play/play/8292...

Source: https://twitter.com/JoyKirr/statuses/352605923828699136

Figure 8.8 Tweet by Hugh McDonald

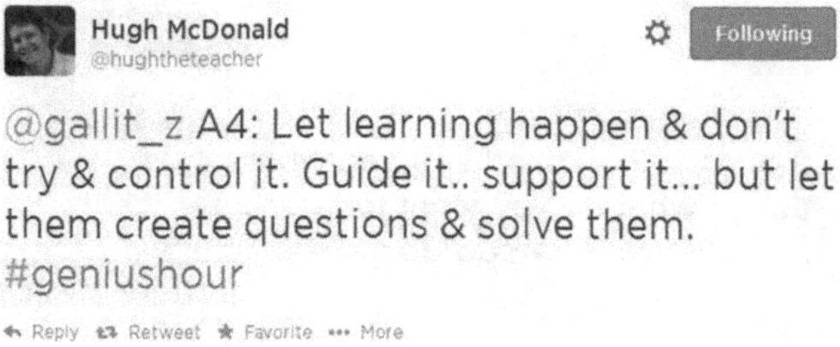

> **Hugh McDonald**
> @hughtheteacher
> ⚙ Following
>
> @gallit_z A4: Let learning happen & don't try & control it. Guide it.. support it... but let them create questions & solve them. #geniushour
>
> ↩ Reply ⇄ Retweet ★ Favorite ••• More

Source: https://twitter.com/hughtheteacher/statuses/352606173809229824

Figure 8.9 Tweet by Robyn Thiessen

> **Robyn Thiessen**
> @RobynThiessen
> ⚙ Following
>
> Go for it! Jump, you will never look back! #geniushour
>
> ↩ Reply ⇄ Retweet ★ Favorite ••• More

Source: https://twitter.com/RobynThiessen/statuses/352606230080000001

Figure 8.10 Tweet by Lindsey Bingley

> **Lindsey Bingley**
> @lbingley
> ⚙ Following
>
> A4: Don't worry if it doesn't go as planned 1st time. Kids need time to get used to this style of learning, too. Keep trying! #geniushour
>
> ↩ Reply ⇄ Retweet ★ Favorite ••• More

Source: https://twitter.com/lbingley/status/352606431926693888

Students Weigh In: Why Genius Hour Matters to Them

Students shared the following:

- ◆ I was able to learn about what I am interested in, not what we have to know and teachers going, "cram cram cram." I learned some of my writing limits.
- ◆ I enjoyed Genius Hour. I think it taught us that we as seventh and eighth graders can change the world with our genius.

- I liked that we were able to do whatever we wanted to try to contribute to the world.
- I really enjoy getting to work with my friends, trying new things on the computer, having our own independent time to work. The best part of this session was acting and filming our video.
- I like that we are given plenty of time to get everything done.

Scrapbooking and photo organizing project

- It was fun; we created some really cool things. I thought of things that I might never have thought of writing about.
- What I like most about Genius Hour is that you can do whatever you like, from videotaping to coloring to learning about a new program. You can always learn something new in Genius Hour.
- I wanted to quit [my Genius Hour project] so bad but I learned that I needed to rise up from the ashes and become bigger and better than I ever thought I would be . . . But I am glad I stayed and in the end I was better than before.
- I really want to hope that someday every teacher could let their children do these wonderful activities that we have done.
- My advice to new Genius Hour students and teachers is to always have something to do and don't give up. Take the opportunity to learn what you want to learn.

Here's another student's take:

> I love when my teacher Mrs. Krebs gives a chance to do Genius Hour. I feel Genius Hour is a privilege so I do not take it for granted.
>
> Genius Hour is an experience to develop new ideas. A chance to be creative and learn what you want to learn.
>
> Genius Hour is important because not many chances do you get to learn things that you want to learn, not what teachers make you learn and then quiz you over it.
>
> Advice I would give to new people would be to do something that you want to do not what others want you to do, not what teachers want you to do, what you want to do. As long as you are being productive and being a genius with your decisions.
>
> Since I am in Junior High I know what it is like trying to survive in a big school with upperclassmen. My friends and I chose to make a video about how to help Junior Highers survive Junior High.
>
> This video includes tips on how to get through Junior High. These tips are school survival tips including the basic teachers, hallways, crushes, etc.[2]

We end with this beautiful quote from student Melina Louise[3] on learning the way her brain understands best.

> For so long I have been told what to know and taught how to know it, but never once did I really feel in control of my learning. It felt like the knowledge went into my brain, stayed there until after my exams, and then was thrown away like a smooth stone into a lake, out of my reach forever.
>
> But when you are passionate about something and can learn it the way that *your* brain understands it, it seems the knowledge takes root.

Add Your Own Voice to the Movement!

Thank you for taking the time to hear all these stories. We absolutely love Genius Hour . . . but now it is up to you. Hopefully, after all those testimonials, you are going to do it. Jump in and give it a go! You will not regret it.

Once you get started, we hope you love Genius Hour as much as we do, and please remember: you are not alone. You have an abundance of resources at your fingertips. In Appendix C, we have included a great reading list that you may want to explore as you move forward. Plus, we have created a website especially for you, the readers of this book. It's at www.geniushour-guide.org, and you will find all kinds of supplemental materials and ongoing updates. You have chosen to start (or continue with) Genius Hour at the perfect time—there is an abundance of information, helpful links and pictures out there. We are thrilled that there are so many resources available nowadays—that means more and more students are getting the opportunity to be creative and to explore their passions and wonders. But, please, don't stop with enjoying the resources.

We need you, dear friends. As you set out to create Genius Hour in your classrooms, please add your own voice to the global conversation about Genius Hour. We need you to *become resources* for others because together we are smarter. It is time for you to share *your* genius in your own schools and with the world. Use all the social media you love and celebrate by posting all the wonderful projects and work of your students. However, we want you to dare to do more than that. That is, to tell your own story. Share how your own learning and teaching craft are being honed through the process and products of Genius Hour. We want to hear about your journey.

Tweet out your blog, videos or other posts to the amazing #geniushour community on Twitter. You can tweet using the hashtag at any time, or join the scheduled chats in two hemispheres (information on http://geniushour. wikispaces.com). Please add your own documents, stories and resources to our collaborative Genius Hour wiki. Or let us know if you would like to cross blog your story to the collaborative blog: http://geniushour.ca.

For those of you that are Pinteresters, a quick search for Genius Hour will show you a ton of great pins. And check out the Facebook Genius Hour group.[4] There's an active community there too.

We truly cannot wait to hear all about the genius of your students and you.

Summary

Teachers all around the world have told us that their classrooms are now changed because they have implemented Genius Hour. And the students feel the same—they love having the autonomy to choose what they are going to learn about. Hopefully you feel ready to start Genius Hour with your class and, when you do, we really hope you will share your pictures, stories and successes with the rest of the online Genius Hour community. We can all benefit from each other's genius. Time to jump in!

Notes

1 http://tinyurl.com/GHSolarz
2 http://tinyurl.com/GHSurvivalGuide
3 http://tinyurl.com/GHMelina
4 http://tinyurl.com/FBgeniushour (Facebook Group). Originally: www.facebook.com/groups/557319844327083

Epilogue: Connecting with the Authors

You'll never know everything about anything, especially something you love.

Julia Child

We invite you to connect with us online. We both love Twitter (that is how we met and how we discovered Genius Hour) and we look forward to connecting with you there. Gallit tweets at @gallit_z and Denise tweets at @mrsdkrebs.

Once again, thank you for taking the time to read our book—we know there are so many fantastic books on education out there and so we are humbled that you chose to spend time with ours.

Afterword

Denise and Gallit (@mrskrebs and @gallit_z on Twitter) were my mentors when I was starting Genius Hour with my seventh graders. They didn't warn me about possible pitfalls; they brought to the forefront the possibilities of children's ideas. I never heard mention of any students struggling with this idea of self-directed learning. They never warned me that other teachers would think I'm crazy. I was surprised when the teacher across the hall would give me a dirty look and shut the door because my class was getting loud. Why keep this information to themselves? I know why now. It's *okay* to fail. Failing at something you're passionate about just gives you more fuel to make it work. It's *okay* for others to look at you as if you're crazy, or "too loud." That means you are engaged. That means you are *trying*. We need to experience this so when the students experience the same, we are ready to support them.

Gallit and Denise talk about autonomy, mastery and purpose. Yes, students are more engaged when these three are in place. What's more, it's the same for teachers. Once you have the autonomy to begin something like Genius Hour, you already have the purpose, and you will want to master it. Each week you will be tweaking ideas and figuring out how to help your students to the best of your ability. Once you see the struggles and the outcomes, you will find ways to integrate student-directed learning into the rest of your week. Your week will become infused with student choice, and student voice.

Is this the end? No. As Denise and Gallit have already said, Genius Hour is only the beginning. It is not the "cure all" for education. It is a baby step, and part of the journey to flipping your classroom on its head, and handing the learning over to the children. Your brain must be spinning with ideas, so it's time to get started on this journey. Hold on for the ride. As you plan, share with the students, facilitate the process and come across issues, reach out to Denise and Gallit. They will be excited to help you on your journey. You'll soon be wanting—and then searching out ways—to implement Genius Curriculum 100% of the time.

Joy Kirr (@JoyKirr), Seventh-Grade National Board Certified ELA Teacher; Genius Hour Thought Leader and Blogger at http://geniushour.blogspot.com

Appendix A: FAQs

Why call this Genius Hour? They aren't really "geniuses."

We don't use the typical definition of *genius* that takes into consideration only a number on the Stanford–Binet Intelligence Scale. Instead we turn to the Latin root of the word genius[1] meaning "generative power" and "producing." Children are generating something new, something innovative. They are producing something for their own purposes. They are creating their own projects and bringing things into being that were not there before. They are being creative and productive. In our view, they are being and sharing genius. And, of course, you can call Genius Hour whatever you and your students like. It's the process of authentic learning that is important, not the name.

Why do we need to teach creativity? Aren't people just born with it or not?

Sir Ken Robinson explains in *The Element* that when someone doesn't know how to read and write, we don't assume they are incapable of literacy. Instead we know that they haven't yet learned how to read and write. In a similar manner, he explains, when students aren't creative, we should not assume that they are incapable of creativity. We should know they just need to be taught. We strive to nurture and grow creativity during Genius Hour.

Don't we have enough to do with the Common Core and other mandated standards?

Of course, there is always so much to do, but to take learning to the next level, which is just what the Common Core is asking of our students, we need learning experiences like Genius Hour. Genius Hour is the perfect way to lead students to new learning. Students love learning about the things they wonder and care about, and this leads to learning with purpose—a much more authentic learning experience. Students flourish when they belong and have freedom and fun in their learning. We have found that when students are empowered they make good choices and enjoy learning. Genius Hour is an excellent way to practice and master many of the Common Core State Standards, or other district, state or provincial standards. See Chapter 6 for some examples.

What is the teacher's role during Genius Hour?

The teacher is the facilitator during Genius Hour. During this time, it is our job to ask the right questions. For the most part, we are not teaching/giving information during Genius Hour, but we are facilitating by asking the right questions to help students keep learning. You may find that you are tired after a Genius Hour session—that is because it is very likely that you will be running all over the classroom: asking questions, giving feedback, chatting with students, doing quick one-on-one checks, admiring work, etc. We have heard of teachers, though, who do their own inquiry or creation during Genius Hour. It's never been an option to us, though. If you are available to them, there will be rich and valuable interactions with your students during Genius Hour. (See Chapter 1 for testimonies of teachers making rich connections with their students during Genius Hour.)

Who should teach Genius Hour?

Teachers and students in every subject area are having Genius Hour. Some teachers ask students to find an inquiry question that relates broadly to the subject area they are studying—math, science, social studies, language. It is exciting to see that students can find something they love in their subject area. They never before knew they had a love for math, until they began experimenting with ratios in using recipes in the kitchen. Or they realize a passion for geometry when they draw tessellations during Genius Hour. Almost everything can be related somehow to social studies, math, science or language. However, because the content is not the major focus, but rather inquiry, creativity and metacognition, most teachers allow students in their content areas to study anything for Genius Hour.

We know of teachers from kindergarten through college classes who are giving students time to own wondering and inquiry, helping students develop their passions. In addition, teachers of special education (see Jason's story in Chapter 3, which shows how much it is needed in the special ed. class), regular education and enrichment/gifted classes are doing Genius Hour.

What are some of the projects that students do during Genius Hour?

Throughout the book, you saw evidence of many of the projects our students have done for Genius Hour, but here are a few examples:

◆ research on content areas of wonder or passion;
◆ stop motion animations;[2]
◆ inventing a new sport;
◆ doing IT work, updating all the computers (see photo below);
◆ crocheting, cross-stitching, sewing;
◆ cooking and baking for families in need;
◆ science experiments;
◆ projects that promote happiness—"Honk if you love someone" event before school and "Take what you need" posters.

Of course, these are just a few of the unlimited ideas your passionate students will pursue during Genius Hour.

For this Genius Hour, he was the go-to IT guy for getting the computers updated

What if a student just wants to be a helper with a classmate's passion?

For a few students, Genius Hour is overwhelming. They seem to cry out: "Too much freedom; just tell me what to do." They don't mess around really, but they don't seem able to take hold of the learning for themselves. Typically, we see these few outliers partnering up with other students who have an idea. The more reluctant one acts as a helper of sorts for the other student's learning. They sometimes want to switch alliances as they lose interest in their first partner or group. They are engaged, but not fully engaged in their own passionate work. (This is different from what we also see—two or three students with the same passion joining forces for a group project.)

We think some students just need more time in unlearning the "school game." Most of our students continue to grow up in a system that rewards them with grades. Alfie Kohn explains in two of his lectures that *No Grades + No Homework = Better Learning*. According to his website, "research consistently finds that giving students letter or number grades leads them to think less deeply, avoid challenging tasks and become less enthusiastic about whatever they're learning—and that's true for those who get As as well as Ds."[3] No wonder some of our students are confused and disengaged when they first begin Genius Hour!

In an attempt to alleviate the problem of the two or three students in a class who struggle finding their passion, one thing you can do is ask them to brainstorm what they love to do, what they are good at and what they wonder. (You can find a "Getting Ready for Genius Hour" brainstorming sheet in Appendix B.) Keep working with them until they are willing and able to list just enough "genius" ideas to find their passion. The lists become great conversation starters about what topic a learner might choose for Genius Hour.

Denise's favorite example is about someone who was a great helper to so many of his friends. He was always in the thick of other people's Genius Hour, and they loved having him because he was a capable and willing helper. However, he had yet to come up with his own project. For one of their Genius Hours, she challenged him to find his own project by brainstorming his interests. He came up with a very short list that included hydraulics. "Hm . . . well, how about learning about hydraulics?" he was asked. He went right to work. Watched a few videos. Found some automotive tubing and syringes. Built the wooden frame at home. Then he wowed his classmates and teachers. His project has been used as an example to many Genius Hour students.[4]

Can I use Genius Hour as a reward for worthy students?

No, please don't. We do not believe that Genius Hour should ever be used as a reward for good behavior or completed class work. Just as all students get to participate in reading, writing, math and science learning, all students should participate in Genius Hour. In fact, Genius Hour may be the key part of the week that inspires your reluctant learners to discover they are truly capable, creative and love to learn. All students need Genius Hour!

What if students like my assignments better than their Genius Hour projects and would rather work on my engaging class projects instead?

It sounds like you are probably a facilitator of learning with your students, helping them solve real and relevant problems. Your question brings up a problem we wish all educators had. It is a great place to start because your students are experiencing engaging school throughout the week. However, you definitely will still want to give them time for Genius Hour.

You ask what if they "like *my* assignments better . . . ?" but what they don't learn from *your* great projects is how to take complete ownership of their learning. They need autonomy. They need to learn the hard work it takes to inquire, develop a plan, work on it, fail forward and carry on through hard times. As Ewan McIntosh[5] puts it, "The world needs a generation of problem finders." They don't need to solve teachers' ready-made problems. They need to find their own problems, make their own decisions. They need time to fail, fall down, pick up the pieces and try again. This will help them own their learning. They need Genius Hour, where the teacher, even you, gets out of their way. That's what is going to help them grow to be lifelong learners, preparing them for life in a collaborative and creative working environment. It may very well be true that 80% of your week is better than Genius Hour for some of your students. That is certainly not to say they don't need that 20% to create, produce and make learning their own.

We would also challenge you to consider giving students more time and choices in your other 80% time. The goal is for students to make learning their own. "Just like design thinking, [with] project-based learning, or any hands-on activity, the value of the experience is diminished when you over-structure and over-plan it," says Sylvia Martinez.[6] So, perhaps a little less structuring on your part will give them permission to find their own problems.

What are some ideas to get administrators on board for Genius Hour?

Honestly, we have been fortunate enough to both work with wonderfully supportive administrations, and so we didn't have to get them "on board" because they were already supportive of innovative teaching and risk taking in our classrooms. However, that being said, if we did have to get approval or sell the idea of Genius Hour, here are some things we would consider:

◆ Tell them about all of the curriculum and competency connections that Genius Hour hits upon (we told you a bit about how it fits in with the US Common Core and BC new draft curriculum in Chapter 6).
◆ Tell them about how Genius Hour fits in perfectly with the ISTE standards for twenty-first-century students (see Chapter 4).
◆ Invite them into your classroom to see Genius Hour in action. We think this is really the best way to get others on board. Once they see how engaged the students are and how motivated everyone is to learn, they will surely be won over.

Explain your rationale. We explained ours at the beginning of the book. Use the same points because, if we are doing Genius Hour right, we are doing exactly what we ought to be doing as teachers!

How can we get parents to buy into Genius Hour?

This is a very important question. Teachers need to answer this question because parents will want to know what is going on. When Denise's class was doing Genius Hour occasionally, it was well accepted. When she went to Genius Hour once a week, she got some pushback from a few parents. She had to go back and better explain the rationale and benefits of doing Genius Hour; this helped the parents to accept the new schedule. For the very purpose of helping the parents of her students understand and buy in to the important work of Genius Hour, Joy Kirr created the go-to Genius Hour resource in Live Binder.[7] Kevin Brookhouser was proactive in answering possible parent questions and concerns before his students even began their 20% projects. His letter[8] to students and parents has become a very popular blog post to guide other teachers in creating their own letter to parents.

What about Genius Hour in the primary grades (K–2)?

What goes on in kindergarten classes around the world, or any early primary grade really, is already much more inquiry-based than it is for their older counterparts. Where else do you get to squeeze Play-doh between your fingers while you think of what you are going to sculpt that day, or put on dress-up clothes and act out dinner time at the house center? Primary students learn through play and we love that. We want more of this in our middle-school classrooms. More freedom to explore and be creative. We acknowledge that our primary friends are learning in a semi-Genius-Hour-type way already.

That being said, primary teachers have asked us how to implement Genius Hour in their classrooms. Ask any kindergarten or first-grade teacher who has tried it, and they will tell you it's not as simple as telling your students they can learn whatever they want for the next hour.

First, as with all age levels, we suggest establishing rapport with your children and strengthening routines in your classroom. At the same time, nurture curiosity and wonder. Welcome questions, dive into inquiry, and laugh, learn and love with your students.

After building rapport, establishing routines and building love of learning with your students, start "Genius Hour" with a group project replete with choices and high interest. Choose a topic that has captured children during regular school-day activities. Gather resources for them to peruse. Or survey students with the simple question, "What do you want to learn?" and then choose a popular idea from their responses. Tell the students they are going to do a group "Genius Hour" and that they can learn whatever they want to within the general topic. Help them develop inquiry questions. See where Genius Hour goes from there. See Figure A1.1 on the next page for a handy infographic.

I teach at a high school. Could I try this there, too?

Yes, definitely. Many high school students are participating in extensive Genius Hour projects. Some teachers call this learning Genius Hour and some teachers call these projects some form of Google's 20% time (20% Time, Google Time, 20% Projects) because they give students one day a week, which usually translates to one class period, or 20% of their time together, to work on their projects.

Passion projects in high school typically extend for one semester or the entire school year. Some teachers grade the projects, but many give full credit for the process of learning, because failure in the project is definitely an option,

Figure A1.1 Genius Hour in primary classes

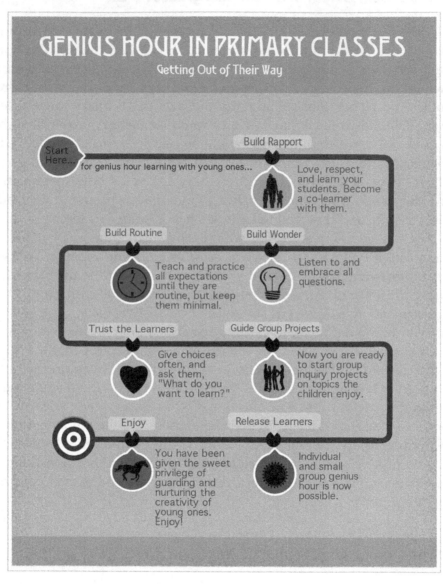

Source: Denise Krebs, made on easel.ly

according to Kevin Brookhouser. Some teachers, like A.J. Juliani, Technology Staff Developer in Ambler, Pennsylvania, and author of *Inquiry and Innovation in the Classroom*, do not grade the final project, but grade checkpoints along the journey, such as blog post updates, reflection pieces and journals.

A popular presentation tool in high schools is the TED-Talk-style presentation. Students present a short, well-polished live presentation explaining their Genius Hour project. They are viewed by parents, fellow students, community members, mentors and teachers. Brookhouser's[9] students in California have created many of these presentations, which have also been taped and posted on YouTube. Besides helping other students around the world be inspired for their own Genius Hour projects, these exemplary videos are an excellent addition to the students' digital portfolios.

Nicholas Provenzano, the Nerdy Teacher, had his students hold their own official TEDx event at Grosse Pointe South High School in Michigan.[10]

High school teacher Valerie Lees[11] has had so much success with Genius Hour at her school that they have even turned it into a locally developed course at their high school. That means students can literally take Genius Hour as a course. How cool is that?

Should we really take our educational cues from the corporate world?

Our inspiration comes from the human world—the world of human motivation—not corporations. Researching and citing 40 years' worth of motivation studies, Daniel Pink has reported succinctly that what motivates us is autonomy, mastery and purpose. Genius Hour provides students with autonomy, time to master and purposeful learning. Those things are motivating for all humans, whether they are young learners in school or adults in the work place.

It seems like Google has begun to rethink giving their engineers 20% of their time to work on their own innovations because limited marketable or "genius" projects result. Why should we continue to do it in schools?

When we started Genius Hour with our students in 2011, we did not have expectations that they were going to create necessarily "genius" products. Our expectations were that students would learn to learn, grow in creativity and produce. That's all!

Giving students time for Genius Hour is a way to begin to *create a climate of creativity*. It's not about *expecting* students to create works of genius, which we would then set against some personal standard of what is genius enough.

Only a small percentage of students are ever going to produce amazing "genius" inventions in elementary or high school. Our students are not *all* going to be the next Albert Einsteins or Marie Curies or Steve Jobses or Grace Murray Hoppers. However, they can all grow more ingenious, inquisitive, original, flexible, adaptable, persistent, willing to take risks and able to live with ambiguity. If given enough time, they can become an expert in something they love, which leads to even more creativity, and possibly to genius inventions and problem solving further down the road.

Promoting Genius Hour begins to stop the insanity of coloring in the lines and getting candy for doing worksheets and lining up in straight rows and doing only what the teacher says.

We need Genius Hour for our kids, not because Google or 3M does it. It's not about taking products to market, as it is for these companies. In fact, even in the corporate world, "genius" ideas are few and far between. Carney and Getz at the *Wall Street Journal* report, "According to academic research, a company, on average, needs 3,000 ideas to get 300 of them formalized, 125 of them into small experimentation, 10 of them officially budgeted, 1.7 launched—and *one* that makes money."[12]

Just as the 3,000 ideas in a company are needed, all student Genius Hour projects are needed. Those that fail to meet a teacher's expectation of creative genius are the good seeds of creation—the creation that may help a child become passionate enough to brave the arduous journey to genius, like Einstein, Curie, Jobs and Hopper did before them.

We are making citizens who can contribute and make a difference in the world. Genius Hour gives students and teachers the gift of time to learn to be creative and remember their earlier love for learning.

Give students a class period, an hour or 20% of their time to learn like this and watch the learning in the other 80–95% of your week grow and blossom.

What about Genius Hour for educators?

We love Genius Hour for our students, but we all know that teachers are learners too. In fact, most great teachers identify as lifelong learners, so we love the idea of Genius Hour for educators. Genius Hour for teachers is a lot like the more well-known, self-directed professional development.

Connected educators have long known the value of Genius Hour: autonomy, mastery and purpose. Teachers, administrators and other instructional leaders spend countless hours on evenings, weekends and summer days learning how best to meet the needs of their students. This kind of personalized learning environment, enlarged by social media, gives connected educators professional development of their own choosing. They are busy in classes, webinars and conferences worldwide. They read volumes of blog posts and watch hours of professional videos.

In addition, outside of pedagogical learning, educators are working on a myriad of passion projects of their own. They come back to school the next day and share with their students the amazing things they've learned. The learning is contagious. See Figures A1.2 and A1.3 for examples of how folks are sharing their Genius Hour projects on Twitter.

Jesse McLean in Alberta does Innovation Day with his teaching staff. We love this idea! Teachers get together for a day of learning and instead of listening to a presenter (what we would normally do on a professional development day, right?), they have what he calls "Educator Innovation Day." In his blog, "Opening Doors and Turning on Lights," Jesse explains:

> The idea behind Educator Innovation Day is twofold: 1) to explore ways to improve education by pursuing a project that you are passionate about and 2) to live the innovative, risk-taking experience so that when we have our students undergo a similar experience, we can speak from a place of understanding rather than just conjecture.[13]

Figure A1.2 Tweet by Laura Verdiel

Laura Verdiel
@Edu_Laura

☼ Following

Starting my own #geniushour project tonight! Excited to share with #imovie soon!

↩ Reply ♺ Retweet ★ Favorite ••• More

Source: https://twitter.com/Edu_Laura/status/334121605766733825

Figure A1.3 Tweet by Craig Dunlap

Craig Dunlap
@Cncdky

☼ Following

While the students work on their #geniushour project, I'm picking up my own passion project. Maybe I can finally finish writing this book.

Source: https://twitter.com/Cncdky/status/552456067893166080

Other schools are experimenting with monthly 1–2-hour periods of Genius Hour for staff development time. Teachers come back to share with their peers what they have learned.

Similarly, during one of Gallit's workshops on Genius Hour (at a typical professional development style event), she gave her attendees time to do a little of their own Genius Hour during the afternoon. Why? Well, like Jesse, we believe that teachers should probably try everything we ask our students to do, and also because it is fun. There were so many educators at her workshop who had a passion for gardening—it was fun to watch them learn something new.

Notes

1 http://tinyurl.com/etymologygenius
2 http://tinyurl.com/StopMotionCar
3 http://tinyurl.com/GHKohn
4 http://tinyurl.com/GHHydraulicsBlog (be sure to read the comments too).
5 Watch Ewan's TEDx talk: http://tinyurl.com/TEDProblemFinders
6 Sylvia's post: http://tinyurl.com/over-structure
7 http://tinyurl.com/GHLiveBinder
8 http://tinyurl.com/20TimeLetter
9 http://tinyurl.com/20Time2014
10 http://tinyurl.com/TEDxGPSHS
11 http://tinyurl.com/GHLees
12 http://tinyurl.com/WSJideas
13 http://tinyurl.com/GHMcLean

Appendix B: Genius Hour Resources and Lesson Plans

Resources

1. Getting Ready for Genius Hour: Brainstorm and Find Inspiration (link to online version: http://tinyurl.com/GHbrainstorm) (see Table A2.1)
2. Genius Hour Creativity Rubric (link to online editable version: http://tinyurl.com/GHrubric) (see Table A2.2)
3. My Genius List of Things to Do and Be (link to online version: http://tinyurl.com/GHList) (see Table A2.3)

Table A2.1 Getting Ready for Genius Hour: Brainstorm and Find Inspiration

Things I Love to Do	Things I Am Good At
1.	1.
2.	2.
3.	3.
4.	4.
5.	5.
6.	6.
7.	7.
8.	8.
9.	9.
10.	10.
Things I Love to Learn	**Things I Wonder**
1.	1.
2.	2.
3.	3.
4.	4.
5.	5.
6.	6.
7.	7.
8.	8.
9.	9.
10.	10.

Table A2.2 Genius Hour Creativity Rubric (genius = creating and producing; that's from the original meaning of the word.)

Quality	Yes, I'm getting it! (5)	Where are you on the continuum between "Yes, I'm getting it!" (5) and "Not yet!" (1)					Not yet! (1)
Ambiguity – I'm OK with a little confusion, knowing there is more than one way to do the job.	I don't need to ask the teacher a lot of questions. I can think for myself and get the job done.	5	4	3	2	1	I have to be told exactly how to do every job. There is only one right way to do the job.
Inquisitiveness – I ask questions and want answers.	I am curious and I look up things that interest me. I'm a lifelong learner.	5	4	3	2	1	I don't ask questions just for the joy of learning, and I don't really want to learn new things.
Generating Ideas (brainstorming) – I create lots of possible ideas.	I am able to fluently create a list of ideas. I use my imagination.	5	4	3	2	1	I cannot see beyond the obvious ideas. I am easily frustrated. I may be lazy.
Originality of Ideas – I create unique ideas! I'm not afraid of what others might think of my ideas.	I can think outside the box and I have a great imagination. I think of ideas that others never even thought of.	5	4	3	2	1	I can only think of ideas that others thought of first. I don't like new ways of doing things. I just want to stick with the old way.
Flexibility/ Adaptability – Mentally, I can bend easily any which way and not break.	I can think of new ways to do things when I get stuck. I can recognize other people's good ideas.	5	4	3	2	1	I am not willing to change my ideas or think of better ones.
Self-Reflection – I can look honestly at myself and evaluate my work.	I can honestly go through my work and know what's right or wrong.	5	4	3	2	1	I lie about my work. I can't or won't look honestly at the things I do well and the things that need more work.

(continued)

(continued)

Quality	Yes, I'm getting it! (5)	Where are you on the continuum between "Yes, I'm getting it!" (5) and "Not yet!" (1)					Not yet! (1)
Intrinsic Motivation – I want to do it. I know the purpose and it pleases me.	I want to try new things. I believe in myself.	5	4	3	2	1	I'm not willing to try new things unless I get something for it.
Risk Taking – I'm not afraid to try something difficult for fear of failure. As Edison said: "I have not failed . . . I have succeeded in proving that 1,000 ways will not work."	I'm not afraid to try anything even if I don't do well at it. I keep trying and find a new way that might work.	5	4	3	2	1	I don't try new things for fear of failing. I try a couple times and give up altogether.
Expertise – I am proud and thankful to know a lot about one or more subjects. I am an expert.	I know I am good at one or more things, and I am not afraid to share my knowledge with others.	5	4	3	2	1	I don't try to be expert at anything. I don't want to be. Or I pretend to not know anything.
Persistence – I can stick with a project even when it gets hard. I understand that the word passion comes from the base word for "suffering."	When the going gets tough, I work harder. I have grit, determination and perseverance. I want to keep going and finish a difficult task.	5	4	3	2	1	I usually quit when I run into a snag. I switch Genius Hour projects often, whenever it gets too hard.

Getting ready for Genius Hour . . . What question do you want to answer? What do you need to do to get ready? How can your teacher help you get ready?

Table A2.3 My Genius List of Things to Do and Be

Directions:

Add your ideas for Genius Hour. You may not get a chance to work on all of these, but at least your ideas will be safe for later when you can work on them.

◆ What are you truly interested in producing and creating?
◆ How will you create, contribute, communicate, connect, collaborate or curate?
◆ Remember, you are a genius, and the world needs, expects, demands and appreciates your contribution!

Idea	Why?	Date finished	Where have you shared your final product?

Lesson Plans

We have included a few lesson plans that you may find helpful. In all of our lesson plans, we make suggestions of what you can say or do, but please remember what we said in Chapter 2—teaching is deeply personal and you have to make this your own. These are only suggestions to help you get started or if you feel stuck, and by no means are the only way to approach your introduction to, or scaffolding during, Genius Hour. You know your students best and you have to do what works for your learners. Pick an entire lesson, part of one or re-invent it in your own way. Have fun with it!

1. Getting Inspired and Beginning Our Genius Hour Wall: Part 1
2. Getting Inspired and Beginning Our Genius Hour Wall: Part 2
3. What Is Genius?
4. How to Ask Good Questions
5. Using Bloom's Taxonomy to Ask Deeper Questions

Lesson Plan 1

Getting Inspired and Beginning Our Genius Hour Wall: Part 1

Learning Intention:

◆ I will be inspired to begin to generate a list of my own passions, interests and wonders.

Assessment Evidence:

◆ List of Genius Hour ideas.

Materials:

◆ *The Most Magnificent Thing* (picture book)
◆ Projector and computer
◆ Internet
◆ Sticky notes
◆ Space for a "Wonder Wall" or "Genius Hour Wall."

Timing:

◆ Approximately 60 minutes.

Learning Plan:

◆ Hook: Read the picture book *The Most Magnificent Thing*, and discuss. Talk about how awesome it is that this little girl is working on her own inventions—she wants to make magnificent things. You may want to also take the time to talk about some of her character traits that are important (her persistence, ability to take risks, etc.). Tell the kids that you were inspired and you want them to have time to be creative and maybe make magnificent things too. Discuss.
◆ Tell the class that there is another person you know that is making magnificent things and show the YouTube clip of Kid President's Pep Talk.[1] Discuss his message of being awesome. Ask the class questions like, "What could we do that would be

awesome?" and give them some time to discuss as partners or small groups.

◆ Watch the YouTube clip Creativity Takes Time[2] and discuss the difference between the work the kids did in the first part and the work that they did in the second part (art was more creative, they had more time to express themselves, etc.).

◆ Tell the students that you agree with the video and think that creativity does take time. Show them your enthusiasm and let them know about Genius Hour. You can say something along the lines of: "And so I am so excited to let you know that I will be giving you that time! Every week we are going to do something called Genius Hour, and we are all going to take an hour to work on something we are interested in or passionate about for a whole hour. That will give us lots of time to be creative." At this point, your students may be shocked, confused, excited—each class reacts differently. Take the time to discuss and get them excited.

◆ Let students think to themselves about what they would do with that time. How would they want to show their creativity? What things are they interested in?

◆ While students are thinking for a moment to themselves, hand out sticky notes to each table group and tell them that if they have any ideas they can begin to record them (alternatively you could use a Genius Hour notebook, journal or lined paper, and students could generate lists there instead).

◆ Have a few students share some examples and share some of your own—the teacher is the chief learner and this is a great opportunity for you to model your wonders and passions.

Lesson Plan 2

Getting Inspired and Beginning Our Genius Hour Wall: Part 2

Learning Intention:

◆ I will be inspired to begin to generate a list of my own passions, interests and wonders.

Assessment Evidence:

◆ List of Genius Hour ideas.

Materials:

◆ Projector and computer
◆ Internet access
◆ Sticky notes from last time (or list in journal) and blank sticky notes
◆ Space for a "Wonder Wall" or "Genius Hour Wall" (or if you are recording in notebooks, then the students will need to have those notebooks out).

Timing:

◆ Approximately 60 minutes.

Learning Plan:

◆ Accessing prior knowledge: Ask the class what they remember about the last time we talked about Genius Hour. Have students summarize and recap what Genius Hour is and some of the ideas from last time. Ask if anyone thought of anything new to add to the Genius Hour ideas wall since last class. Give them a minute to share with the person sitting beside them and perhaps share one of your own too.
◆ Tell them that today you are going to watch a few more inspirational videos and you are going to continue to brainstorm ideas on the Genius Hour Wall.

◆ Watch the YouTube video called Caine's Arcade[3] and discuss as a class. Students will probably say that he is creative; try to push their thinking and get them to describe what characteristics are creative, or what it is that he does that makes him creative. Make the connection to what Caine does to the girl in *The Most Magnificent Thing* and to Genius Hour (he had an idea and built something like her, they had time to work on projects that were interesting to them, etc.).

◆ Watch another short YouTube clip, Obvious to You, Amazing to Others.[4] Hand out sticky notes to each table group and discuss: "You may still be holding back ideas that are fantastic because you think they are too obvious." Talk about how "we all feel like that sometimes and so even ideas that you think are just ordinary or not exciting should be written down on the sticky notes too. All ideas are good and should be recorded. Sometimes we just don't know that our Genius Hour ideas are genius!"

◆ Give them a bit more time to think, write and discuss. During the discussion you can make connections to what they already had up on the board, celebrate new ideas, etc. Remind them about Kid President's video and encourage them to think about ideas that help make the world more awesome. Have them add all their interests and passions.

◆ Closure: Invite the class to stick their new sticky notes to the Genius Hour wall (or Wonder Wall, or section of the room where they can be displayed). If you don't have wall space, you can have kids record in their own notebooks and then discuss in small groups or share with the whole group (either in discussion format or as a Gallery Walk).

◆ Invite the class to keep thinking of ideas and to keep recording them, and tell them that next Genius Hour class you are going to start developing those ideas into their own Genius Hour project ideas.[5]

Lesson Plan 3

What Is Genius?

Learning Intentions:

- ◆ I will know various definitions for the word "genius."
- ◆ I will know that I can consider myself "genius" in some way.

Assessment Evidence:

- ◆ Student participation
  - o during Inside/Outside Circles
  - o in creation of exit slip.

Materials:

- ◆ Paper and drawing materials for each student
- ◆ A variety of dictionaries and thesauruses (online or hard copies)
- ◆ Exit slips with question, "What is one time I've done something I might consider *genius* (or other words we've looked at, like artistic, creative or productive)?"

Timing:

- ◆ 30–45 minutes
- ◆ I would teach this lesson if you and your class plan to call your autonomous learning block Genius Hour.

Learning Plan:

- ◆ Hook: Write the word "genius" on the board. Have students quickly sketch out a picture or words that illustrate the word *genius*. Don't give any more instruction than this. Have students share their images or words with a partner. Have some of the students share their ideas with the large group.
- ◆ Someone is sure to mention the IQ test or 150 IQ or any such reference to the Stanford–Binet Intelligence Scale. Please tell

them that, today, they are going to look at everything but that definition of genius.

◆ Share the learning intentions and tell the students that today you will explore the word genius, and how you, the teacher, believe that they have genius, and you are hoping over the next days and weeks, they will come to believe it too.

◆ Let the class choose whether they will work alone or with a partner or two, of their own choosing.

◆ Have students find "genius" in one of the word resources. Ask students to be on a word hunt for how they themselves may have been or will be described as genius. For instance, one of the synonyms for genius in Thesaurus.com is perspicacity, which may make a student click on it because he doesn't know what it means. Then he discovers it means *discernment, shrewdness, understanding*. He continues to click on those words, follow that vein of *genius*. Now, this child may know he is really good at understanding and retelling jokes, he's appreciated for his sense of humor and he notices puns and double meanings in language. He can begin to get the idea that this could be a form of genius. Another student will discover the word *dexterity*, and know that genius can relate to her ability to consistently win medals during track meets. Another discovers that his *artistic* strengths can be considered a form of genius. Another has an unusual *knack* for cooking. Another works hours every week and has a strong *ability* as a skateboarder. Another has an *aptitude* for math. We believe every person has forms of genius that need to be identified and developed.

◆ Next, do Inside/Outside Circles. Split the children into two equal-sized groups. Group A stands in a circle and then Group B makes a circle around Group A. Group A turns to face Group B so now everyone is matched up with a partner. Group A completes one of more of these sentences to Group B.

   o A synonym for genius that I learned is _____.
   o Something I am good at is_____.
   o Something I love to do is_____.
   o Something I like to learn is _____.

Then Group B completes one or more sentences talking to their partner in Group A. Group B takes a step to the right (so that everyone has a new partner) and repeats so that they can have a discussion with a new partner.

◆ Come back to the large group and hear a few students share their synonyms and thoughts with the large group.

◆ Here is where you can take time to share your favorite definition of genius. My favorite is from an original meaning: "generative power." I like to tell my students that being genius is using their talents and perseverance (power) to generate, which literally means to create or produce. (A special thank you to Laura Coughlin for introducing us to this definition of genius. See more here: http://tinyurl.com/etymologygenius.)

◆ Remind students of your learning intentions. Your goal was for them to learn a broader definition of genius than a number on a test. Second, it was for them to consider that they have some aspect of genius in them.

◆ Closure: Give students an exit slip and have them answer the question: "What is one time I've done something I might consider *genius* (or other words we've looked at, like artistic, creative or productive)?"

Lesson Plan 4

How to Ask Good Questions

Learning Intentions:

- ◆ I will know the difference between Google-able questions and non Google-able questions.
- ◆ I will be able to ask good inquiry questions (for my Genius Hour project).

Assessment Evidence:

- ◆ Student participation
    - o during Think/Pair/Share
    - o in creation of sticky-note wall
    - o during Inside/Outside Circles.

Materials:

- ◆ Sticky notes
- ◆ Bowl with random topics in it (for example: flowers, cars, clouds, soil, rainbows, Hawaii, forests)—things they will know a few facts about
- ◆ Chart paper for an anchor chart (or you can do this on the board)
- ◆ *Stella: Princess of the Sky* (this one is great for younger students; you could choose any picture book that introduces questioning/has a curious main character). Adrienne Gear has loads of examples in her book *Reading Power*.[6]

Timing:

- ◆ Depending on the age of your students, this lesson can probably be completed in a 45-minute period (perhaps a bit longer for younger learners who need more time to write)
- ◆ I would teach this lesson during Step 2, before Step 3 (after I have introduced the concept of Genius Hour and we have brainstormed our passions, but before we have come up with our specific inquiry question) *or* after we have completed a round of Genius Hour already and I want my students to start to think deeper about their questions.

Learning Plan:

- Hook: Read the picture book *Stella: Princess of the Sky* by Maire Louise Gay, and talk about how her brother, Sam, asks so many questions.
- Share the learning intentions and tell the students that today we are going to talk about questions and how not all questions are the same. Some questions are really easy to answer, like "What day is it today?" and some are meatier, like "What is your favorite day of the week and why?" Some teachers refer to these as skinny and fat questions, thin and thick questions, Google-able and non Google-able,[7] questions you can ask Siri and questions you can't ask Siri, shallow and deep, etc.
- Pick the wording you would like, share an example or two and have students Think/Pair/Share about what they think the difference is between the two types of questions. Give them roughly 30 seconds to think to themselves first and then ask them to turn to a partner and discuss for two minutes. Pick several students to share what their duo talked about and discuss as a class. Record what they are saying on a T-chart on the board or on an anchor chart for future reference.
- After you feel like you have enough information on the T-chart to summarize the differences, put students into groups of 3–4 and tell them you are going to practice asking skinny vs fat questions (or whichever phrasing you have chosen).
- Prepare ahead of time a bowl with a bunch of random topics on small slips of paper and have students pick out one slip each. In their small groups, they have to brainstorm a bunch of skinny questions and a bunch of fat questions for each topic they have collectively picked. They can write the questions onto sticky notes and then put them up on a vertical surface (bulletin board, white board, etc.) under the correct heading on a large T-chart (i.e. one side says thin questions and one side says thick questions). Give students enough time to brainstorm the questions, write them down and stick them up on the vertical surface.

- ◆ Once done, go through them as a class and decide as a large group if they are in the correct category. Discuss and make any changes that you and the class think are necessary.
- ◆ Closure: Inside/Outside Circles. Have the students split into two groups. Group A stands in a circle and then Group B makes a circle around Group A. Group A turns to face Group B so now everyone is matched up with a partner. Group A tells Group B one thing they learned today. I usually refer back to the learning intentions and remind the class what the point of the lesson was. Then Group B tells about one thing they learned. Group B takes a step to the right (so that everyone has a new partner) and we repeat so that they can have a discussion with a new partner.

Lesson Plan 5

Using Bloom's Taxonomy to Ask Deeper Questions

Learning Intentions:

◆ I will understand Bloom's taxonomy and the six levels of questions.
◆ I will be able to ask questions for each of the six levels of questions.

Assessment Evidence:

◆ Students will have example questions for each of the six levels on Bloom's taxonomy and will have recorded these questions onto chart paper.

Materials:

◆ Several picture books
◆ Chart paper on which students can record their questions.

Timing:

◆ Depending on the age of the students, this lesson will take approximately 60 minutes.
◆ I would teach the previous lesson on questioning first and then do this as a Part B to that introductory lesson on questioning.

Learning Plan:

◆ Accessing prior knowledge: Ask students what they recall about our last questioning lesson (see lesson plan above) and do a quick recap of thick vs thin questions.
◆ Explain that there are actually several different kinds of thick and thin questions and that a lot of people use something called Bloom's taxonomy to categorize questions.
◆ Show an overhead or screenshot of the Bloom's taxonomy pyramid and explain that there are six levels: Remember, Understand, Apply, Analyze, Evaluate and Create. Take a

few minutes to go through them all and explain them to the class. Doing a quick Google search of Benjamin Bloom (creator of Bloom's taxonomy) or simply Bloom's taxonomy should bring you to a bunch of great visuals that you could show the class. I also like the ones that give links to question starters. Again, just type in Bloom's taxonomy questions and you will get some great examples to use.

◆ Model the different types of questions by connecting to something you are doing in social studies or science and creating questions for each level. (I could go through some, but I think it is much more beneficial to use this as an opportunity for cross-curricular connecting and so I will leave it to you to pick how to do this. If you are studying plants in science, use plants as an example; if you are learning about Ancient Rome in social studies then perhaps use that. It is up to you!)

◆ Put students into groups of four and ask each group to pick a picture book. (You could line up a bunch of options on the ledge of the board at the front, or put a few choices onto a side table.)[8]

◆ Once they have picked a book, the students need to read the picture book together and then, using the picture book as the content, come up with a good example of a question for each of the six categories.

◆ Using chart paper, record each question and what level of Bloom's taxonomy it corresponds to. (Give them a few different colors and let them be creative in how they chose to visually represent this.)

◆ Have students display their chart paper along with the picture book that they used and then do a Gallery Walk as a class so that students have a chance to see the work of their peers. Variation: You could also have students do a quick share to the whole class *or* they could pair up with another group and share with each other.

◆ Closure: Let students know that all of the six levels are important depending on what you are doing but that for Genius Hour you are focused on meatier questions. Ask students which levels they think would work best for a Genius Hour project. Discuss as a class. Let them know that soon you will be going back to the passion/wonder board so they can pick their first Genius Hour inquiry question. Leave them excited to do more!

Notes

1 http://tinyurl.com/GHPepTalk
2 http://tinyurl.com/GHTime
3 http://tinyurl.com/GHCaine
4 http://tinyurl.com/GHObvious
5 You may want to watch a few more inspirational videos listed in Chapter 2 over the next few days and keep adding to the list before Step 3 (developing the inquiry questions). This will probably depend on how many ideas the students were able to generate. We like to spend a few weeks on Steps 1 and 2 (getting inspired and brainstorming), so do not feel like you need to rush to the part where they develop their own questions. We also recommend going outside for a nature walk, if that is an option. Students can record questions and wonders and add them to the Genius Hour Wonder Wall too.
6 www.readingpowergear.com
7 Thank you, Lindsey Own, for sharing your "Google-able" vs "non Google-able" wording with us. Lindsey first learned about this from http://notosh.com.
8 Thank you, Kam Grewal, for sharing with us your idea of using picture books to teach questioning.

Appendix C: Genius Hour
Reading List for Educators

Books

1. *Who Owns the Learning?* by Alan November
2. *The Passion-Driven Classroom: A Framework for Teaching and Learning* by Angela Maiers and Amy Sandvold
3. *Classroom Habitudes: How to Teach 21st Century Learning Habits and Attitudes* by Angela Maiers
4. *Drive* by Dan Pink
5. *The Element: How Finding Your Passion Changes Everything* by Sir Ken Robinson
6. *Creating Innovators: The Making of Young People Who Will Change the World* by Tony Wagner
7. *Essential Questions* by Grant Wiggins and Jay McTighe
8. *Inquiry and Innovation: Using 20% Time, Genius Hour and PBL to Drive Student Success* by A.J. Juliani
9. *Mindset: The New Psychology of Success* by Carol Dweck
10. *ROLE Reversal* by Mark Barnes
11. *The 20Time Project* by Kevin Brookhouser

Blogs

1. *Ask What Else* by Sheri Edwards (https://askwhatelse.wordpress.com)
2. *My Own Genius Hour* by Joy Kirr (http://geniushour.blogspot.com)
3. *Mrs. Thiessen's Grade 3 Class Blog* by Robyn Thiessen (http://mrstsgrade3sclassblog.blogspot.com)
4. *Today Is a Great Day for Learning* by Hugh McDonald (http://hughtheteacher.wordpress.com)
5. *ComPassion Based Learning* by Oliver Schinkten (http://compassionbasedlearning.blogspot.com)

There Is No End to Education

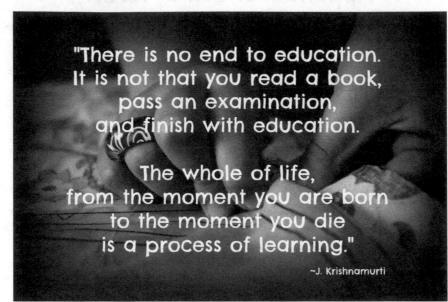

Source: https://www.flickr.com/photos/mrsdkrebs/10191190673

Picture Books to Use When Introducing Genius Hour

1. *The Most Magnificent Thing* by Ashley Spires

   This is such a great picture book starring a little girl and her dog/
   assistant on her quest to create the most magnificent invention. The
   journey isn't perfect though and she "fails" quite a few times. This
   book is perfect for teaching persistence, risk taking and flexibility—all
   traits that are on the Genius Hour rubric that we use. This book would
   be beneficial right at the beginning, after you introduce Genius Hour
   and are about to get started.

2. *What Do You Do with an Idea?* by Kobi Yamada

   In this story, a little boy has an idea (represented as an egg) but he
   doesn't know what to do with it. He carries it around for a long time
   until he finally learns that ideas are meant to change the world. This
   picture book would be perfect for taking Genius Hour from inquiry-
   based and passion-based learning to the level of compassion-based
   learning! Perhaps one to consider after your class has done a round of
   Genius Hour and you want to bring back the discussion on making a
   difference in the world.

3. *Iggy Peck, Architect* by Andrea Beaty

   This picture book is about a little boy named Iggy Peck and his passion for architecture. It is such an enjoyable read and would be great to introduce the concept of passion as well as for understanding the intrinsic motivation trait on the Genius Hour Creativity Rubric. The book can also be used to share with students how sometimes our Genius Hour projects can be about building, creating or inventing something (helpful if your students are stuck on research-only type inquiry questions).

4. *Rosie Revere, Engineer* by Andrea Beaty

   Rosie is a fantastic character. She loves making things and embodies so many of the characteristics that we would attribute to Genius Hour and the Maker Movement. Rosie is inspired by everything around her. This book can be used to introduce the discussion on inquisitiveness, risk taking and generating ideas. It also teaches an important lesson about failure and persistence.

5. *Q is for Question* by Tiffany Poirier

   Need help thinking about *big* questions? This picture book, written in ABC format (A is for Answers, B is for Beauty, C is for Cause, etc.) can help us think about our questioning. We would suggest reading this book to the class but also making sure that it is on-hand for students to flip through when they need inspiration as it is a lot to take in after only one read-through. Poirier encourages us to have philosophical discussions and debates with our students, and we think this book is a great place to start those discussions. This book connects to inquisitiveness and generating ideas on the Genius Hour Creativity Rubric.

6. *The Dot* by Peter Reynolds

   This is one of Reynolds' many fantastic picture books. The book begins with a little girl, Vashti, sitting in her classroom with a blank piece of paper on her desk. Her teacher encourages her and says, "Just make a mark and see where it takes you." Vashti gives the paper a "good, strong jab" and leaves it with just the dot. She returns to the classroom on another day and finds that her teacher has framed her dot. Vashti is then inspired to do even better on her next picture. Some of our students may have a hard time getting started on projects, and if you have one of these students in your class then this might be a good book to use as there are many connections between Vashti's journey and the Genius Hour journey.

7. *It's Okay to Make Mistakes* by Todd Parr

This picture book helps us learn that it is okay to make mistakes, and that sometimes things do not go quite the way we thought they were going to, but that is part of trying new things. "It's okay to make mistakes sometimes. Everyone does, even grown ups! That's how we learn." Exactly! And this is an important thing to learn if we are going to do Genius Hour. You can use this book to talk about risk taking and self-reflection: two of the many traits on the Genius Hour Creativity Rubric. This one is probably best suited to younger students.

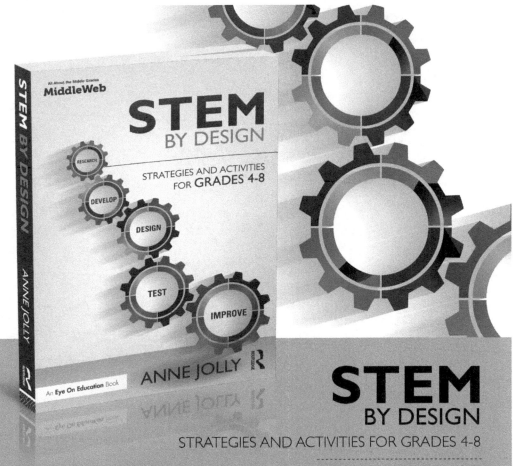

STEM
BY DESIGN
STRATEGIES AND ACTIVITIES FOR GRADES 4-8

© 2016 • 978-1-138-93106-0 • $34.95

Figuring out how to design effective and engaging STEM activities can be challenging. In this much-needed book, popular STEM blogger and consultant Anne Jolly provides practical, clear advice that will help you get started or expand your current program. A co-publication of Routledge Eye On Education and MiddleWeb, Jolly's book covers everything from what makes a lesson truly STEM to how to fine-tune the STEM learning experience in ways that will increase student achievement. Throughout each chapter, you'll find a variety of engaging lesson ideas, activities, tips, and resources. Bonus activities are available as eResources on our website so you can download them for classroom use.

ANNE JOLLY is a curriculum consultant for a Mobile-based, NSF-supported project to develop engaging, standards-based STEM lessons for middle schools. Her popular MiddleWeb blog STEM By Design currently offers more than 100 articles and represents a valuable resource for teachers and leaders. She began her career as a lab research scientist, made the shift to middle school science teacher, and is a former Alabama State Teacher of the Year.